Devotions with a Difference

Devotions
with a Difference

by
Stephen and Janet Bly

MOODY PRESS
CHICAGO

Library of Congress Cataloging in Publication Data

Bly, Stephen A., 1944—
Devotions with a difference.

Summary: Presents devotions and related Bible verses
on sixty-two alphabetically arranged topics from Anger to
Zeal.
1. Youth—Prayer-books and devotions—English. [1.
Prayer books and devotions. 2. Alphabet] I. Bly, Janet. II.
Title.
BV4850.B55 1982   242'.63   82-8304
ISBN 0-8024-1789-2

5 6 7 Printing/AF/Year 87 86

Printed in the United States of America

for Russ and Mike

Contents

1

Anger

"Be angry, and yet do not sin; do not let the sun go down on your anger, and do not give the devil an opportunity" (Ephesians 4:26-27).

Joyce slammed the door on Danny. Dave yelled at the umpire. Cindy screamed at her little sister.

Do Christians ever get angry? Yes.

Should they? Only on rare occasions.

For two years straight, Joyce has had to sit in front of Danny in algebra class. Danny quickly grasped all the new concepts after just one try. But he had an annoying habit of putting down all the kids who couldn't keep up with him, and that usually included Joyce.

By the time the mid-semester algebra II final rolled around, Joyce prepared to get even. She studied extra hard so she would get at least as good a grade as Danny, if not better.

The day of the test, Danny walked into class and announced to Joyce that he hadn't studied at all. Joyce was sure she had him this time. But the next day, Danny shoved his paper onto her desk. He had a bright red $A+$ next to her $A-$. Then he had the nerve to say how easy that test was. Joyce never said a word. She quietly picked up her books and strolled over to the door, then out to the noisy hallway. She could see Danny just steps behind her, then—slam!

Dave wasn't having a good day, either. He was up in the bottom of the ninth with two out, yet he hadn't had a hit all day. Suddenly his luck seemed to change. A hard-hit ball down the third-base line seemed to mean a sure double. As he approached second, he knew the ball was coming in for a close play. He hit that base with a head-first dive. "Out!" yelled the ump.

Dave couldn't believe it. He had made it. And that play would make or break the game. But arguing did no good. The game was over. Dave stormed off the field.

Cindy walked into her bedroom just in time to catch her six-year-old sister, Brenda, sitting in the middle of her bed with her jewelry scattered all over. Cindy yelled at Brenda, "If there's anything missing or broken, you're in for it!" And she yelled at her mother, "Tell Brenda to stay out of my room! That's the third time this week she's messed up my things."

Anger is all around us. Anger is that strong expression of displeasure that, uncontrolled, can explode into physical or verbal demonstrations of rage. Most times, explosions of anger are harmful. Here's why.

We lash out in anger when we're frustrated because we've been denied something we want. Joyce wanted the highest grade. Dave wanted that double. Or anger springs up when someone or something interferes with the controls we want on our lives. Cindy hadn't planned on spending thirty extra minutes untangling her necklaces and chains. And her right to privacy had been violated, too.

Anger

Anger is also a defense or excuse when we've failed to take an honest look at our own abilities. Dave considered himself a good hitter. But some days he just couldn't hit as well. This may have been one of those days.

Dave also may have honestly believed that he beat the tag at second base. It's easy to get angry when we think we see, or we're the victims of, injustice.

But are these things worth the wear and tear that anger puts on our bodies, our personalities, and our families and friends?

The Bible says, "Be angry, and yet do not sin." So, there must be times when it's right to show anger. Jesus gave us a few examples. He got angry when His Father's house was misused (Mark 11:15-17), when the helpless were taken advantage of (Mark 3:1-5), and when so-called religious leaders kept people from true knowledge of God (Matthew 23:13-36). But even in those cases anger was meant to be a warning, a motivating factor for change.

A good goal would be to practice control of anger-producing situations. Save anger for worthy causes when it can be used as a tool for righting wrongs rather than as a cover for personal weaknesses.

Also check out: Bitterness, Forgiveness, Frustration, Jealousy, Motives, Pettiness, Pride, Self-control, Violence.

2

Apathy *

"But He said to him, 'A certain man was giving a big dinner, and he invited many; and at the dinner hour he sent his slave to say to those who had been invited, "Come; for everything is ready now." But they all alike began to make excuses. The first one said to him, "I have bought a piece of land and I need to go out and look at it; please consider me excused." And another said, "I have bought five yoke of oxen, and I am going to try them out; please consider me excused." And another one said, "I have married a wife, and for that reason I cannot come"'" (Luke 14:16-20).

The folks in the above passage suffered from apathy. Apathy is indifference, a lack of interest. When a person is apathetic toward spiritual matters, apathy can be as dangerous as a chronic disease.

Every Sunday morning, you can find Terry Hatfield in one of the Santa Clara Community Church restrooms. No, he's not sick. He's just skipping Sunday school. His parents make him go, but he just isn't interested. He used to blame Mr. King.

Mr. King had taught the high school class for over twenty years. Terry thought he was boring. He thought Mr. King was just too old to relate to the things Terry was interested in. But Mr. King retired from the class on his sixtieth birthday. That's when Bart Traylor took over.

Mr. Traylor was in his twenties and the assistant football coach at Houston High. Sunday school began to change. The class centered on discussions of dating, drugs, and what happens when we die. But Terry still hides in the men's room. He had to finally admit he wasn't interested no matter what they talked about.

Apathy is also a form of selfishness. It's a statement to the people around you that they aren't worthy of your attention. That kind of attitude quickly stifles growth of any kind.

Try this short test. Think carefully of every bit of knowledge that you have learned through someone else. Include everything from math equations to throwing a curveball. Now imagine that all that accumulation of abilities were unexpectedly taken away. What would you have left?

We all need input from other people to make our lives richer. Apathy cuts us off. And apathy to spiritual truth could be a matter of life and death, our eternal destinies. That was true in the story Jesus told in Luke 14.

There are cures for this condition. One way is to develop a frontier explorer frame of mind. Consider each day a potential adventure. You never know when you're just moments away from meeting an important new friend, learning a vital, exciting truth, or receiving some other special surprise. In fact, every day can be like a surprise party when the Lord God of the universe is your Father.

Apathy can be a bad habit that needs to be broken. A habit of skipping Sunday school needs to be turned around.

For Terry, breaking that apathy will be awkward the first time or two. But he would want to do it if he ever gave God's Holy Spirit a chance to stir him alive inside.

Also check out: Boredom, Depression, Disobedience, Friends, Future, Purpose, Selfishness, Ungratefulness, Zeal.

3

Atheism

"The wicked, in the haughtiness of his countenance, does not seek Him. All his thoughts are, 'There is no God'" (Psalm 10:4).

The cafeteria buzzed with the usual lunch-time chatter. Kristina Ward grabbed her tray and steered toward a half-empty table. She wasn't eating with Mindy and Sylvia today, because she needed to study her notes for the drama test next period.

As she spooned into the usual Friday "Oh Boy Chili" and enchiladas, she opened her binder. But she found it hard to concentrate on the various quotations from Shakespeare's plays that she would need to identify. A group of noisy kids down the table interrupted her thoughts.

"Well, I'm surprised that anyone in this day and age would even step inside a church," a girl Kristina recognized as the head majorette was saying. She pulled back a long strand of thick, blonde hair. "I learned long ago that there's no Santa Claus, no Easter bunny, and no bearded man in the sky named God."

"Yeah, who needs it? Rules, rules, and more rules. As Mr. Baum says, our society has outgrown its need for religion. We can do what we want, when we want, and not

17

worry about guilt trips." Martin Lanning, with the tightly curled hair and deep brown eyes, winked at the majorette. "Isn't that right, Suzanne?"

Suzanne giggled. "Hey, Martin. You having another party this weekend?"

"I sure am. Saturday night, same time." He waved to the others sitting with them. "You're all coming, aren't you? *Everybody* will be there."

Kristina is a junior at Will Rogers High School, a typical American public school. Sometimes it seems to her that she is the only Christian on the campus. That isn't true, of course, Mindy and Sylvia are Christians, and so are a lot of others if Kristina took the time to count them. But Will Rogers school is so big, and there are so many students and teachers who talk like Suzanne and her friends, that Kristina can't help but be discouraged at times.

How can they be so blind? she wondered. *Why can't they see the plain evidence of God at work in the world around them? Why aren't they afraid to make fun of the Lord God and His people?*

Kristina committed her life to Christ three years ago through the witness of Mindy and Mindy's mother. Three years later, she was still realizing how much she had yet to learn about being a faithful follower of Jesus Christ. Sometimes there were tough times of obedience and painful times of discipline. The constant pressure of contacts with unbelievers added to this made Kristina really think. *Is this the best way to live my life? Am I missing out on all the fun? What if there really is no God, no Jesus who rose from the dead? What a fool I'd be.*

A few days after overhearing Suzanne and Martin, Kristina ate with Mindy and Sylvia out on the school lawn. She told them what she had been feeling.

"Kristina, it's good for us to have our faith tested," Mindy answered. "We need to know that we'd choose Christ even if it means not being a part of Suzanne's gang or going to Martin's parties. And speaking of Suzanne, you never once mentioned the possibility of what will happen to her if *she's* wrong and you're right. She has everything to lose. Her life is on a dead-end street."

Then Sylvia said, "Why don't we pray for Suzanne and her friends? Let's ask God to provide some way that each one of them can have an opportunity to hear about His love and care for them."

"Operation Suzanne" went into effect that day. At the end of the school year, the three girls took an inventory of the results. Although there was no evidence that Suzanne seemed any closer to acknowledging God's existence, she and Kristina had had several good talks and now knew one another on a friendly basis. But the big news was that Martin, the perpetual party-giver, had begun coming to their church youth group events and had talked with their youth pastor about an openness to commit his life to Christ.

Besides that, the year of praying together about specific needs had strengthened the girls' faith. They now looked at Will Rogers High as an exciting mission field rather than as a dreary, daily confrontation.

Also check out: Boldness, Creation, Doubt, Friends, Judgment, Materialism, Peer Pressure.

4

Bitterness

"See to it that no one comes short of the grace of God; that no root of bitterness springing up causes trouble, and by it many be defiled; that there be no immoral or godless person like Esau, who sold his own birthright for a single meal" *(Hebrews 12:15-16).*

How could he dare do it? Andrea thought as she fumed inside the locker room. She paced the tiled floor, up and down, up and down. Her white gym uniform was ringing with sweat. Then, she suddenly burst into tears. She ran for her towel and furiously wiped her face.

What am I going to tell Mom? she asked herself. Just that morning she had assured her whole family that this year she wouldn't be cut from the basketball team. After all, hadn't Coach Perry told her just last week how much she had improved? But there was the list posted again with no mention of Andrea. Andrea did notice one thing. There was Bernice Daggett's name right on the top line. Even thinking the girl's name caused a hot rush of blood to Andrea's cheeks.

"Well, Bernice, you did it again," Andrea said to the empty room as she changed into her street clothes.

Andrea had known Bernice since the sixth grade, when

they were both students in Mrs. Hanson's class. Mrs. Hanson had been a P.E. major in college and always seemed so impressed with Bernice. Bernice could run faster, throw farther, and jump higher than any girl in the school. Not only that, but she also let you know that she knew she was better. Last year when the basketball team had been announced, Bernice had smiled in that smug way of hers and ran out on the court to shoot a perfect basket from the top of the key.

Andrea hopped on her bike for the long, hot ride home. The tears rolled down as she thought about how she hated Coach Perry, how she hated Mrs. Hanson, and especially how she couldn't stand Bernice Daggett.

Then she felt the unmistakable thump, thump of a flat tire. *That figures,* thought a miserable Andrea. She stopped and pushed out the kickstand. A piece of glass had cut a gash right through the tube. As she was looking at it, Andrea heard a male voice close behind her and raised up with a start.

"I think I have a tube that size on an old bike. You're welcome to have it," the boy said. Andrea recognized Mike Burnett from her English and French classes. He was walking with his younger sister and his girl friend, Martha. All Andrea could think about at that moment was seeing Bernice walking around the campus with Mike and Martha lately. That was enough for her.

"Thanks, but no thanks," she replied curtly. "I can take care of myself, if you don't mind."

Mike looked at her a moment, then shrugged and took Martha's hand. "Sure, Andrea, just thought I might help," he said.

Andrea walked the bike slowly home. Now she not only had to tell about the basketball bad news, but she also had a bike to get fixed. It was either that or ride the bus to school. There was no way she wanted that. Bernice rode the same route she would have to take.

Andrea was tempted to call Mike Burnett. But she just couldn't make herself dial his number. *I'd have to apologize, for one thing*, she reasoned. *And I don't really know him all that well, for another. But I sure do need that tube. It's all Bernice's fault.*

Several months later, Andrea joined a Bible study group with five kids from her church. One of the early lessons dealt with what the Bible calls a "bitter spirit." Through the lesson, the truth hit her about her relationship with Bernice. She was astounded to realize what a far-reaching, harmful complication this root of bitterness made for her life.

She made a decision to forgive Mrs. Hanson, to forgive Coach Perry, and to forgive Mike, Martha, and several others she had added to her hate list since then. Finally, the big one, she tried to forgive Bernice. A four-year-old habit isn't easy to break, but Andrea determined to make things as right as she could.

Most of all, Andrea asked God to forgive her for resenting the people and circumstances He had brought into her life for His special purposes.

Also check out: Anger, Criticism, Failure, Jealousy, Love, Restitution, Self-worth.

5

Boldness

"Now it came about after the death of Moses the servant of the LORD that the LORD spoke to Joshua the son of Nun, Moses' servant, saying, 'Moses My servant is dead; now therefore arise, cross this Jordan, you and all this people, to the land which I am giving to them, to the sons of Israel. . . . Only be strong and very courageous; be careful to do according to all the law which Moses My servant commanded you; do not turn from it to the right or to the left, so that you may have success wherever you go'" (Joshua 1:1-2, 7).

As soon as Brad spotted Marshall and Raney, he knew he had trouble. Brad darted across the dark school courtyard and tried to ignore the staggering silhouettes that converged on the sidewalk ahead.

But Raney grabbed Brad by the jacket. "Listen, snake," he threatened. "If you say one word about this, you'll wind up with two broken legs."

Brad pulled himself away and hurried in the direction of his home. That's when he saw it. Sprayed across the brand-new gymnasium was a collection of red obscenities aimed at the high school principal. The paint was still wet.

What would you do if you were Brad?

Forget the whole thing?

Write an anonymous note to the school board?

Try to clean off the paint?

Report the incident immediately to the police?

Laugh and add a few words of your own?

Brad chose to flag down Lieutenant Carpenter and report the vandalism. Marshall and Raney were caught and suspended from school. Now Brad dreads going out at night. Raney's threat unnerved him. Often, boldness reaps unwanted consequences.

Boldness is a positive, courageous action in the midst of threatened negative results. Here's a boldness self-test you can take:

	Yes	No
1. The most important goal for me at school is to make and keep friends.	_____	_____
2. I'm often embarrassed to admit to certain people that I'm a Christian.	_____	_____
3. I act differently at school from the way I do at church.	_____	_____
4. I'm waiting until later in life to be a witness for Christ.	_____	_____
5. As long as life goes smoothly for me, I try not to get involved.	_____	_____

The "yes" answers are a sure sign that you need a boldness booster.

Joshua sure did. He was scared. Moses, his leader for the

past forty years, had just died. Joshua needed an instant boldness booster course. And that's just what God gave him. Take a look at all he was offered in Joshua 1. That formula can work for us, too.

First, recognize and accept the present difficulties. For Joshua that meant a wide river to cross, fierce enemies to defeat, and a fickle multitude to lead.

Second, obey God's Word as you know and understand it. Joshua was commanded to obey God in every detail that he had learned from Moses.

Third, relax. The rest is up to God. The Lord promised to reward Joshua with success. Our God enjoys honoring those children of His who remain faithful during difficult situations.

Also check out: Apathy, Compromise, Failure, Fear, Future, Inconsistency, Peer Pressure, Shyness, Zeal.

6

Boredom

"Jesus therefore said to them again, 'Truly, truly, I say to you, I am the door of the sheep. All who came before Me are thieves and robbers; but the sheep did not hear them. I am the door; if anyone enters through Me, he shall be saved, and shall go in and out, and find pasture. The thief comes only to steal, and kill, and destroy; I came that they might have life, and might have it abundantly'" (John 10:7-10).

"School is boring. TV is boring. Church is boring. Tony is boring. Even listening to my favorite records is a bore." Anyway, that's what Tricia claims.

Boredom is the state of weariness caused by uneventful dullness. Can you imagine a fifteen-year-old worn out because her life is just one big, uneventful dullness?

It takes work to be bored. Modern-day life is crammed with adventure. And the Christian life is the highest adventure of all. Take a good look at those who walked with Jesus. One minute He calmed the sea. Then He cast a demon out of a wild man. Great crowds clamored to crown Him a king. Days later they shouted to crucify Him. Blind men stumbled after Him. Rulers fell before Him. He cuddled small children in His arms and whipped moneychangers in His Father's house.

Jesus' followers were frightened, joyous, overwhelmed, amazed, beaten, and exalted. But they were never bored. Even those who chose to follow Him after He returned to heaven found an exciting life-style. Listen to Paul:

Three times I was beaten with rods, once I was stoned, three times I was shipwrecked, a night and a day I have spent in the deep. I have been on frequent journeys, in dangers from rivers, dangers from robbers, dangers from my countrymen, dangers from the Gentiles, dangers in the city, dangers in the wilderness, dangers on the sea, dangers among false brethren [2 Corinthians 11:25-26].

And he was just getting warmed up. Paul bored? Never! And what about Peter, John, Philip, or Stephen? Were they bored? They didn't have time for a yawn.

Jesus promised an abundant life of meaning, purpose, joy, and surprises. Life gets to be a bore *only when you get too far away from Jesus.* To be with Jesus is to be right in the center of the action. You never know what might happen next.

Life also gets to be a bore *when you ignore others and focus only on yourself.* If I could run away to an isolated cave, away from people and safe from nature's elements, perhaps I could plan out every second of my days. I would always know what's going to happen to me. Absolutely nothing could interrupt my schedule. How boring that would be.

But what if I include some companions, get out in the wind and rain and weather, and go exploring the territory around us? Then the possibilities for adventure are endless.

Also, life becomes a bore *when you're afraid to take risks.*

Boredom 31

A boring life has to be carefully formed and shaped by a sterile mind. No one else can be blamed for your life of boredom. Have you ever risked a challenge in which you might fail? To stay bored is a pretty safe niche. Some people would rather just lie there forever.

Also check out: Apathy, Griping, Happiness, Love, Material-ism, Purpose, Selfishness, Shyness, Zeal.

7

Bragging

"And the Philistine said to David, 'Am I a dog, that you come to me with sticks?' And the Philistine cursed David by his gods. The Philistine also said to David, 'Come to me, and I will give your flesh to the birds of the sky and the beasts of the field.' Then David said to the Philistine, 'You come to me with a sword, a spear, and a javelin, but I come to you in the name of the LORD of hosts, the God of the armies of Israel, whom you have taunted. This day the LORD will deliver you up into my hands, and I will strike you down and remove your head from you'" (1 Samuel 17:43-46a).

That conversation sounds like a lot of hot air. It is true that both David and Goliath were boasting. But only one of the two was just plain bragging. Bragging is exaggerated promotion of one's own deeds in order to put down someone else. It is a common human trait.

When Robert's girl friend, Cathy, talked on and on about how strong her new neighbor was, Robert snapped, "I can press a hundred pounds more than he can any day."

But could he? Robert had no idea. He just felt a sudden compulsion to build himself up in the eyes of his girl friend, even if that required making a rash statement. For some, bragging becomes a way of life. How do you deal with a friend who is that way?

First, try to understand the bragger. People who have a bragging habit really don't like themselves. They assume others won't like them, either, unless they can convince them to believe their propaganda about themselves. They are people who hurt because they have low self-images.

Second, be honest about *yourself*. Show your friend that you joyfully accept yourself, imperfections and all. Demonstrate by your actions that it's OK to be who you are, no more and no less.

Third, don't be afraid to compliment your friend's positive qualities. That's right. Our natural reaction is to snub or humiliate such a person in some way. But that person desperately needs the self-assurance your positive feedback could give. Then he won't need to brag as his self-esteem grows.

There are some things in each of our own lives for which we can take no credit. God has supplied these conditions by His choice. For instance:

God-given	*Learned abilities*
red hair	painting a picture
5'6" tall	rebuilding a cycle
good singing voice	champion chess player
American family	an A grade in chemistry
strong teeth	money saved in bank

We should never boast about those things in the "God-given" column. They are God's gifts to us. We have nothing to say about the matter. But the activities in the "Learned abilities" column show what we've done with what God gave us. Here is where our sense of achievement should come from. Here is where we need to compliment others for their accomplishments, too.

Also check out: Competition, Criticism, Friends, Frustration, Future, Happiness, Humility, Inferiority, Jealousy, Pride, Self-worth.

8

Clothes

"And He humbled you and let you be hungry, and fed you with manna which you did not know, nor did your fathers know, that He might make you understand that man does not live by bread alone, but man lives by everything that proceeds out of the mouth of the LORD. Your clothing did not wear out on you, nor did your foot swell these forty years. Thus you are to know in your heart that the LORD your God was disciplining you just as a man disciplines his son" (Deuteronomy 8:3-5).

How would you like the clothes you now own to last you another forty years and look as good as they do today? Some of you would be delighted. What a money saver it would be. How wonderful it would be to be free from the pains of hours of frustration in clothing store dressing rooms.

Others would be horrified. Worn-out rags are the best excuse in the world to try out the newest fashion style. We live in a culture that constantly strives for the "new look." Last year's wardrobe won't do if you want to be part of the "in" group.

That's what Russell tried to explain to his mother. He couldn't buy just any pants and shirts for school. They had to have the "Lightning Bolt" brand. His mother calmly

What are Some name brands

37

explained that that was out of the question because that brand cost five to ten dollars more per item than his usual, sturdy, department-store choices. But Russell insisted and his mother gave in. Russell proudly marched on campus his junior year with a flash on his shirt collar, a flash on his tennis shoes, and a flash on his back pants pocket.

That summer, Russell got his first full-time job working at the local furniture store. And his mother announced that since he was making so much money, he would buy his own school clothes. Russell was delighted. He kept his eyes alert to his friends. He wanted to be sure to keep up with them when school rolled around. Sure enough, he caught sight of lots of "O.P.s." "Lightning Bolt" was out. "O.P." was in.

By the time the long, hot summer came to an end, however, Russell began to have second thoughts. Why should he spend his hard-earned cash on expensive outfits that he could only wear a few months? He took time to figure it out one night. He could buy almost twice as much if he shopped back at the department store. That's when he decided he'd chance being the class nonconformist.

Russell survived his senior year just fine in his department-store clothes. But many teens wouldn't dare try what he did. Clothes, to them, are the most important representation of who they are.

Does God have any interest in the clothes we wear? What does the Bible say? If sin had never entered our world, we probably wouldn't even bother with clothes. Adam and Eve were naked in the Garden of Eden and weren't the least bit embarrassed about it—that is, until they bit into the forbidden fruit. Disobedience to God somehow caused a chain reaction of not only separation from God's close friendship, but also a break in the easy, comfortable intimacy with fellow human beings. Clothes are a part of that personal privacy we need to work toward whole relationships with those we love.

Later God used food and clothing, both necessities, to discipline the Israelites in their wilderness wanderings. He proved His love and care while also teaching them what their priorities should be by withholding and then abundantly providing those basic needs.

Jesus chided His followers in Matthew 6 for not trusting God to furnish all their material needs, including clothes. He reminded them that this is the same God who created the intricate beauties of all nature around us. That same God understands our desires for attractive things to wear.

If you've always thought of God as an old-fashioned old man who is hopelessly out of touch with modern life-styles and tastes, maybe it's time to commit to Him such details as the clothes you wear. You just might be surprised by how "with it" our all-knowing God can be.

Also check out: Friends, Happiness, Humility, Inferiority, Jealousy, Materialism, Peer Pressure, Pride, Self-worth.

9

Competition

"Do you not know that those who run in a race all run, but only one receives the prize? Run in such a way that you may win. And everyone who competes in the games exercises self-control in all things. They then do it to receive a perishable wreath, but we an imperishable. Therefore I run in such a way, as not without aim; I box in such a way, as not beating the air; but I buffet my body and make it my slave, lest possibly, after I have preached to others, I myself should be disqualified" (1 Corinthians 9:24-27).

Some people fear that competitive sports aren't a good thing for youth. "Teaches kids to put others down. Kids with little skills have their self-image lowered, and undue stress is put upon physical strength," they say.

Those points have merit. But just the same, competition in itself is neutral. It's what a person does with it that matters. And whether it's trying out for a part in the school musical or applying for that job position that just opened up, we can't escape living in a competitive world.

Competition involves physical, mental, or spiritual action with the goal of demonstrating your highest level of achievement in that area. It's much more than merely outdoing someone else. After all, winning isn't everything.

For instance, suppose your high school football team defeated the Kindergarten All-Stars, 276-0. Would you feel a sense of accomplishment? But what if your team played the Dallas Cowboys and Dallas finally won in a sudden death overtime, 34-31? You'd feel on top of the world.

The challenge of competing against someone better than you are will mature your own skills. Whether it's basketball or basket weaving, you're bound to improve. Practice the piano by yourself and you'll just poke along. But practice for a recital and you'll find yourself attempting runs and cadences of which you never dreamed you were capable.

Those who never compete will never know the distress of losing, but they'll also never taste the joy of winning. Nor will they ever experience the high excitement of giving your all to a task in the midst of competing. True satisfaction comes from looking back and knowing you did your best.

Competition also teaches self-control, a valuable fruit of the spirit (see Galatians 5:19-23). Successful competition requires a forceful act of the will and action of the body to complete the required rigors. When the body rules, the mind gives in to "I'm too tired," "I just don't feel like it," "It's too much bother," or "I'd rather have another piece of cake."

Those who receive Christ as their Savior receive the gift of the Holy Spirit. That doesn't mean that a Christian is immediately controlled by God like a remote-control robot. But the Holy Spirit is available to give a special, divine assistance in those areas of our thoughts and actions that need redirection. Therefore, a Christian has a greater potential for discipline and perseverance, necessary tools for any kind of competition.

Also check out: Failure, Grades, Purpose, Self-control, Success, Victory, Zeal.

10

Compromise

"For though I am free from all men, I have made myself a slave to all, that I might win the more. And to the Jews I became as a Jew, that I might win Jews; to those who are under the Law, as under the Law, though not being myself under the Law, that I might win those who are under the Law; to those who are without law, as without law, though not being without the law of God but under the law of Christ, that I might win those who are without law. To the weak I became weak, that I might win the weak; I have become all things to all men, that I may by all means save some" (1 Corinthians 9:19-22).

Compromise sounds like a dirty word to some. There are times when it is bad.

Wendi used to be very particular about the boys she dated. Then she met Brent. She heard from her friends that he had a wild reputation and that he had been kicked off the football team for drinking. But Wendi reasoned, *I'm seventeen now and able to handle myself.*

One night Wendi and Brent ran into some older buddies of Brent's down at the bowling alley. They talked the two into joining them down at the river for a party. When they got there, Wendi discovered they had brought along a case of beer. She had no desire to join in at that point, but she wasn't brave enough to make a scene and force Brent to take her home. So, she suffered through the long hours of drunken brawling and prayed for her safety when she finally got a ride.

Compromise can be good, however. A healthy compromise is giving up something you want in order to settle a difference with another.

Annette and Lydia rarely agree on anything. That's not too unusual for sisters. But their parents had insisted that Annette wash the dishes on odd-numbered days and Lydia on even days. That worked out fine until Lydia was elected to be cheerleader and Annette wasn't. Then Lydia had to practice cheers two nights a week.

Lydia made a suggestion to Annette. "Why don't you wash the dishes every night and I'll make it up when the sports season is through?"

Annette stomped out of the room. "No way!" she replied.

But later Annette cooled off and proposed a plan of her own. "I'll wash the dishes and you clean my room on Saturdays. How about it?" Lydia thought about it and then agreed. It was a compromise.

In First Corinthians, Paul treats compromise as an effective way to bring people to a knowledge of God. As long as his actions did not violate God's laws, he felt free to use many common interests to draw unbelievers into conversation about their need for Christ.

How can you know when compromise is helpful? Generally, compromise is OK if you don't violate a principle you know to be true from Scripture, if such action won't divert you from God-given goals for your life, and if the plan won't hinder another person's spiritual growth.

The important thing is to know what are relatively minor issues and what are the basic morals and creeds you choose to live by. The side issues can be compromised; the morals can't.

Think of a compromise as a sharp kitchen knife. A cook can't get along without one. But if misused, it is a dangerous weapon.

Also check out: Dating, Drunkenness, Friends, Guilt, Inconsistency, Marriage, Motives, Peer Pressure.

11

Creation

"Worthy art Thou, our Lord and our God, to receive glory and honor and power; for Thou didst create all things, and because of Thy will they existed, and were created" (Revelation 4:11).

If there's one thing the Bible says no one can possibly argue about, it's the emphatic claim that God created the material world we live in and everything in it. The Scriptures begin with the startling statement: "In the beginning God created." That theme is repeated over and again throughout the Bible. And for many, this one claim becomes a stumbling block to the rest of God's message.

Fifty years ago, scientists believed they had forever banished those words as hopeless myth. As they began to study new data regarding the universe's mysteries, some interpreted the information to mean that the cosmos always existed and always will. One of the theories proposed was called the "steady-state" theory. At about the same time, anthropologists proclaimed the discovery of another link in the monkey-to-man evolutionary process. They felt that supported their thesis that simple life evolves into advanced complexities. That is, life on our planet keeps getting better and better.

Christians raised an immediate outcry. It seemed that the very core of their beliefs was being threatened. Many denounced those claims in highly emotional speeches and writings. Unfortunately, there weren't many spokesmen for the Bible's view that gave carefully reasoned or thought-provoking counter statements. Christians came under fire as "not living in the modern age" and "blinded by religious myths."

But a strange phenomenon is occurring in our own time. The newest suppositions of science are again causing a dramatic recoil, this time from the scientists themselves. Evidence has been growing for some time that we live in an expanding cosmos that seems still to be experiencing the aftermath of a gigantic explosion or convulsive beginning of some kind. The important point is that these discoveries strongly hint of an instantaneous beginning.

Why should that upset scientists, anthropologists, and atheistic professors all over our country? Because they live by just as religious a supposition as the most zealous Christian. Their creed is: "There is no God. We are the masters of our own fate." They cannot contend with the possibility that they aren't in control. They don't want to come to grips with the incredible chance that there is a Supreme Being out there to whom all this belongs. They explore in order to control, not to give homage to a Controller.

Albert Einstein was just one example of those with that prevalent attitude. When his equations of general relativity were first announced, an astronomer named Willem de Sitter used Einstein's own formulas to predict an exploding universe in which galaxies moved rapidly away from one another. Einstein's reaction? "This circumstance of an expanding universe is irritating. To admit such possibilities seems senseless to me." So scientists are just human beings with pet notions of their own, too, and not the neutral "seekers of truth" we assume them to be.

What, then, do we do in our classroom studies and labs when we clash with philosophies that underly scientific research?

First, let's understand the touchiness on both sides. The basic foundations for life-styles and creeds are being threatened, at least on the surface. But as Christians we can keep calm. God's truth will always remain. Theories will come and go. Even "facts" come and go.

Second, encourage teachers you know to present all the knowledge of our age. Often, only the information that supports one given position is reported in the classroom. That's one of the tendencies that groups like the Creation Research Society are trying to combat.

Third, diligently search the Scriptures as you study the minds of men. Determine your own stand on conflicting issues. And don't forget to marvel at how our ancient documents continue to speak to the deep needs of mankind in all eras, to people of all levels of intellect.

Also check out: Atheism, Doubt, Judgment, Motives.

12

Criticism

"Be patient, therefore, brethren, until the coming of the Lord. Behold, the farmer waits for the precious produce of the soil, being patient about it, until it gets the early and late rains. You too be patient; strengthen your hearts, for the coming of the Lord is at hand. Do not complain, brethren, against one another, that you yourselves may not be judged; behold, the Judge is standing right at the door" (James 5:7-9).

Moses was the most humble man who lived during his day (Numbers 12:3). But his sister and brother, Miriam and Aaron, were upset with him. Who did he think he was? they retorted. Was he the only one who could speak God's words? Numbers 12:1 reveals their true motive. They didn't like Mrs. Moses.

John the Baptist was a man who was filled with the Holy Spirit even before he was born (Luke 1:15). Jesus said that as a man he was the greatest who had ever lived (Matthew 11:11). But that didn't keep Herod's wife from wishing he were dead (Matthew 14:8), or certain critics from suggesting that he had a demon (Matthew 11:18).

Then there was Jesus. Jesus Christ had no faults. He was perfect. Surely no one could criticize Him. But plenty did

(and still do). Some griped that He ate and drank with
sinners. Others complained that He didn't require His
disciples to wash ceremonially before meals. He was often
accused of dishonoring the Sabbath.

Whenever we grumble about someone else, we are really
trying to prove to others and ourselves that that person is
deficient in some area that demands immediate attention.
But most criticism tells us more about the one doing the
criticizing than it does about the one being criticized. In
each of the examples above, criticism was used as a defense
to hide one's own sin, an attempt to keep from dealing with
problems in one's own life.

Of course, there aren't many people like Moses, John the
Baptist, and Jesus around. So, the rest of the imperfect
people we know should be fair game for a close, critical eye,
right? Jeanie used to think that. She doesn't now.

The first week of poetry class, Jeanie was dismayed to
see that she would sit right behind a new student by the
name of Sylvia Stephens. Jeanie didn't know Sylvia. All she
knew was what she could see from the back of her. While
Jeanie tried to concentrate on the lectures on rhyme
schemes and historical periods, her attention kept drawing
back to Sylvia's limp and oily hair. The tag on her dress
stuck out as well.

Jeanie was the kind of girl who glanced in a mirror every
chance she could get. She wanted every hair in place, no
straps showing, and her posture straight as a model's. She
just couldn't understand why this girl didn't try to make a
better impression her first days at school.

Later in the week, Miss Harrison assigned an iambic

pentameter poem for the students to try. Jeanie was frustrated. She just couldn't concentrate with unkempt Sylvia sitting there. Finally, she forced herself to finish the project and jumped up to place the paper on Miss Harrison's desk.

She smiled at Miss Harrison and then turned around. That's when Jeanie noticed the awkward scrawl of Sylvia's writing hand. Her other hand sprawled limply across her notebook. Just under Sylvia's long sleeves, Jeanie could see some kind of braces. Jeanie's shock soon turned to shame. Why hadn't she noticed that before? Her head pounded as she reached for her books.

Then she overheard Miss Harrison as she walked up to speak softly to Sylvia. "Would you mind if I read this poem of yours to the class tomorrow?" she asked. "It's an excellent example of the type of imagery we'll be studying."

Sylvia turned and Jeanie watched her smile out of a charming, pixy-like face. "Sure. But please don't tell who wrote it. I'd be too self-conscious."

The next day, Miss Harrison read a number of student poems. Jeanie had no doubt which one was Sylvia's. It was a beautiful picture of grief and hope, using symbols about an accident in which someone died and someone lived, and it posed a question about what purpose there was for the one who remained. There was an allusion made to the cross of Christ, where He died that many could live.

Jeanie felt her cheeks wet with tears. She leaned over to Sylvia and hugged her. "So you're a Christian, too?" she whispered. "I loved your poem."

It's amazing how Jeanie's perception of Sylvia changed

after that. Jeanie no longer saw just oily hair and tags. She learned her first lesson in seeing people as whole human beings with reasons for what they do.

Also check out: Bitterness, Bragging, Griping, Humility, Inferiority, Motives, Pettiness, Self-control, Ungratefulness.

13

Dating

"Do not be bound together with unbelievers; for what partnership have righteousness and lawlessness, or what fellowship has light with darkness? Or what harmony has Christ with Belial, or what has a believer in common with an unbeliever?" (2 Corinthians 6:14-15).

I talked recently to a young woman who was busy preparing for her upcoming wedding. She remarked that she had had no idea how many details were involved. Then she laughed and said, "I think I'll advise my friends from now on to get started planning their weddings before they go looking for a husband; that's the easy part."

Besides being humorous, that young woman touched on a valid point. This side of the wedding vow, before that serious commitment before God is made, some thinking needs to be done. What kind of family do you want? What type of lifetime companion do you desire? But, you say, I'm not ready for marriage. I just want to date, to have some fun. Your marriage partner will come from one of those dates, however. And the usual rule for our society is, Find someone you're attracted to, then fit your life's goals to theirs.

Well, why not? Isn't that what marriage is all about?

Aren't you supposed to learn to work together with your spouse as a team? Yes. But when it comes to a Christian who is at the stage of making close friendships with the opposite sex, certain ideals need to come above the pull of nature's instincts.

Take a close look at the marriages around you. If you're in the mainstream of life today, you'll find many sad stories. The saddest is of the Christian who is married to an unbeliever. Something has to give. Either the Christian must minimize his or her commitment to Christ, or there exists a huge gap in communication and oneness between the partners. Either way, the individual Christian suffers. The marriage suffers. The children suffer. And the church suffers.

Some tough questions need to be asked back when the involvement and emotional tugs are still controllable.

Do I want to marry only a Christian?

What kind of behavior would I find intolerable in someone I lived with day in and day out?

What qualities are important to me in a future mate?

Do I already have some direction on what God's will for my life is?

Have I considered the possibility that the best plan for me is to remain single?

The give-and-take exchange of ideas and interests that develops from fun times and intimate fellowship times with members of the opposite sex is an indispensable part of our becoming well-rounded people. We need friends whom we consider as close as brothers and sisters. We also need to recognize those of the opposite sex who are best kept at arm's length. Close interaction with them could lead to spiritually stagnant waters. If you determine what red flags to look out for, you're one step ahead of the traps so many fall into.

Also check out: Compromise, Family, Friends, Future, Happiness, Inconsistency, Love, Marriage, Purpose.

14

Death

"But we do not want you to be uninformed, brethren, about those who are asleep, that you may not grieve, as do the rest who have no hope. For if we believe that Jesus died and rose again, even so God will bring with Him those who have fallen asleep in Jesus. For this we say to you by the word of the Lord, that we who are alive, and remain until the coming of the Lord, shall not precede those who have fallen asleep. For the Lord Himself will descend from heaven with a shout, with the voice of the archangel, and with the trumpet of God; and the dead in Christ shall rise first" (1 Thessalonians 4:13-16).

Hank was glad not many guys from the football team were there. He had a reputation for being tough. Standing around bawling like a baby wasn't his idea of toughness.

He had been strong when Dad first told him Grandpa Barnes had died. He knew his grandfather had been seriously ill. They had all been expecting it. But actually being there at the graveside hit him hard. It was all over. That's all there was. There would be no more fishing together at the dock, no more heated games of chess, and no more hearing how things were back in "the good old days."

It didn't seem fair to Hank. *Something's wrong with a*

system in which both good men and bad men wind up the same way, he thought to himself.

Hank's right. Life wasn't originally meant to end with a grave. To fear death is human. Jesus came to deliver us from that fear (Hebrews 2:15). So for Christians, death takes on a different meaning.

For those who believe in Christ, death isn't an end—it's the beginning. A believer just crosses over into eternity. Death is only a gate into that eternal existence.

When believers die, we can relax. They are now in the hands of a loving heavenly Father. Their troubles are over. They made it to the finish line.

Even at the death of one who we are pretty sure didn't trust in Christ, we can still be at peace if we know he had heard the gospel. We can trust that God will deal with him justly. He will receive what he asked for, that is, a separation from God's presence and intervention, if he didn't trust Christ before dying. Also, we can be motivated to tell those around us just what the benefits of knowing and following Christ are, both in this life and in the next.

In the meantime, don't feel foolish about tears at a funeral. We're still going to miss the ones who die, whether they're believers or not. We're still going to have moments of distress about our own impending deaths. But also take some time to give thanks to God. There's more to the story because of what Jesus did on our behalf. Because He lives, we, too, will live.

Also check out: Boldness, Depression, Fear, Illness, Judgment, Purpose, Suicide, Trauma, Victory.

15

Depression

"For even when we came into Macedonia our flesh had no rest, but we were afflicted on every side: conflicts without, fears within. But God, who comforts the depressed, comforted us by the coming of Titus. . . . I now rejoice, not that you were made sorrowful, but that you were made sorrowful to the point of repentance; for you were made sorrowful according to the will of God, in order that you might not suffer loss in anything through us. For the sorrow that is according to the will of God produces a repentance without regret, leading to salvation; but the sorrow of the world produces death" (2 Corinthians 7:5-6, 9-10).

Depression is that inactive doldrum state that is the result of an uncontrolled siege of sadness, rejection, or self-centeredness. Too much time spent in this pit means spiritual, emotional, and sometimes physical trouble.

Certain personalities seem more prone to periods of depression than others—the quiet types, the perfectionists, and also the aggressive, "got to make everyone happy" types. But the good news is that the very ones who are prone to depression are also capable of sensitivity to the hurts and needs of others. All they need to do is to focus their attentions outward instead of always inward.

"Repentance without regret"—what a wonderful state of mind to have. Most depressions have feelings of regret at the roots. God offers a freedom from living with the doom of regrets.

Some depressions are just habitual responses to situations that don't turn out as we want them to. Other depressions can be much more serious. They can be the products of a deeply troubled or mixed-up mind. Perhaps there's some traumatic memory that keeps haunting. Or some evil force plagues any attempts at peaceful living. Those cases may require the help of an experienced counselor.

For the rest of us, dealing with recurring depression takes some stubborn backtalk to our thinking processes. Below are four suggestions for dealing with depression.

1. During a time of reasonable cheerfulness, make a list of subjects that always lead you into a downward spiral of depression. Then, make a promise to yourself: "I will not allow myself to think about _____ anymore." Then tell yourself, "No! Stop!" whenever that thought comes to your mind.

2. Get to a typewriter or find a pen and write down in clear, simple sentences all the reasons why you're depressed. Then force yourself to write at least five reasons why you should *not* be depressed. It's a good idea to have handy a list of the "why not" reasons that you make during one of your "up" times.

3. Force yourself to move your body into a different environment. Get out for a walk. Go play with some children. Take a nap and sleep it off. Go visit a friend.

Attempt something creative like baking a pie, painting a picture, or writing a song.

4. Read through the book of Psalms. You'll be able to relate to David's own depressions in a new way. And don't forget to join in with the hearty praises. Our God is always worthy to receive our sacrifices of praise.

An occasional bottoming out is normal. It can even give us an opportunity for some needed thinking about who we are, where we're going, and what we need to do. But the depression should lead somewhere, get us back on our way, and help us slip back into the mainstream of our assigned duties with a renewed vigor.

Also check out: Anger, Bitterness, Boredom, Failure, Forgiveness, Future, Happiness, Purpose, Self-worth, Trauma, Zeal.

16

Disobedience

"And every one who has this hope fixed on Him purifies himself, just as He is pure. Every one who practices sin also practices lawlessness; and sin is lawlessness. And you know that He appeared in order to take away sins; and in Him there is no sin. . . . By this the children of God and the children of the devil are obvious: any one who does not practice righteousness is not of God, nor the one who does not love his brother" (1 John 3:3-5, 10).

Rules. The world is full of them.

"Don't run in the hallways." "Twenty-five-mile-an-hour speed limit." "Three tardies and you receive a detention. "No street shoes on the gym floor."

One of the dumbest rules to Cherie was that you couldn't leave the high school campus at lunch unless your parents wrote a note. On Friday at about 11:00 A.M., she realized she had left her English report on the kitchen table. Mrs. Malcom wouldn't think too highly of her excuse. She needed that report by 1:10.

Any other day, she would have called her mother. But today was Ladies' Day at the golf course. There was no way to reach her. So, at 12:10 Cherie marched down the Third Street alley, cut across McElhenys' back yard, and ran up her driveway on Black Oak. With paper in hand, she returned by the same route. It was no problem. She made it without being stopped. *It's a dumb rule,* Cheri assured herself again, *especially for seniors.*

It's true that some rules are illogical, ill-conceived, or born out of petty motives. But what does that have to do with obeying or disobeying them?

We can all agree that it is wise to keep rules involving safety. If we don't, someone could be hurt. But how about those rules that don't make sense to us? Is that a time to cut corners?

Consider this: Obedience is a habit. Human beings are not obedient creatures by nature. Anyone who claims otherwise has never babysat two-year-olds. The majority of them challenge every order or suggestion with a firm "No!" The only way we can be confident of keeping to the "straight and narrow" with the major guidelines for life is to have a clean track record in the smaller ones.

Each of us has a diversity of relationships. There is our social circle, our religious circle, our scholastic circle, our work circle, and our family circle. Each of those relationships influences the others. A little disobedience in the home could weaken conduct at school. And the more chips we hack out of the standards of obedience in each of these circles, the harder it will be to obey God.

The Scriptures say that sin is lawlessness. Check yourself out. How do you react to the following question-and-answer test?

Q. What laws should be obeyed?

A. All of them.

Q. Aren't there any exceptions?

A. Only if a law forces you to violate a clear teaching of the Bible.

Q. What if I think a law does violate the Bible? What then?

A. Make certain you have a thorough understanding of that teaching. Approach the ones enforcing the rule with an explanation of your conviction. Respectfully suggest how the rule could be changed in such a way that you could comply. (See how Daniel did it in Daniel 1:8-13.)

Q. What if they are unwilling to compromise?

A. Be prepared to bear the consequences. Take the penalties you had been forewarned about, and do it without complaints.

Q. What if the rule doesn't violate the Bible, but it still seems ridiculous?

A. Obey it anyway. But also work through every available, honorable means to have it changed or abolished.

Also check out: Compromise, Criticism, Lying, Purpose, Restitution, Self-control.

17

Doubt

"The Jews therefore gathered around Him, and were saying to Him, 'How long will You keep us in suspense? If You are the Christ, tell us plainly.' Jesus answered them, 'I told you, and you do not believe; the works that I do in My Father's name, these bear witness of Me. . . . I and the Father are one.' The Jews took up stones again to stone Him" (John 10:24-25, 30-31).

Jesus loves seekers. His heart is always open to those who earnestly search for truth and carefully weigh all the information they're given. We see this when Jesus confronted the rich young ruler, Mary Magdalene, Zacchaeus, and Nicodemus. All those people were seekers.

Then, there are the phony seekers. Jesus ran into plenty of those, too. They would constantly challenge Him to prove He was who He said He was. But when He demonstrated miracle after miracle, they explained each of them away: "He does miracles by the power of Satan." "He can't be from God; He heals on the Sabbath."

Those people even grilled a young man who had been blind from birth and could now see because Jesus had touched him. They wanted to catch Jesus in some infraction of the law, either religious or civil. Never mind that a once-blind man could now see. They bristled at the idea that this nobody from Galilee could draw power and attention away from themselves. He had invaded their territory. They even dared to risk the possibility that they were denouncing a prophet of God. Why? Because they weren't true seekers. They were playing power games.

The idea of seeking brings us to the subject of doubts. Is it wrong to doubt? No, not if the doubter is a seeker who will analyze the evidence and then embrace the truth when it is found. Doubting should lead somewhere. Instead, however, many use doubts as a hedge to prevent an open commitment to anyone or anything. Or, as in the case of the Jews, they used their "doubts" as a public defense against a challenge to their life-styles.

Anyone who truly wants to know if God exists can find out. He is ready and willing to draw close to those who try to come near to Him. He has also left with us a written document of His dealings with His creation down through the ages. This book, our Bible, is filled with assurances that we can know some things to be facts.

We can know that our sins are forgiven (1 John 1:9).

We can know if we really do know Him (1 John 2:3).

We can know false prophets from true prophets (1 John 4:2-3).

We can know if God lives in us (1 John 4:15).

We can know we have nothing to fear on the Day of Judgment to come (1 John 4:16-18).

We can know for sure that we will experience eternal life (1 John 5:11-12).

We live in a very unstable world. Sometimes it seems you

can't depend completely on anything or anybody. So, doubts are natural. Some doubting is almost inevitable.

But there is One who can be trusted, who will never steer you in the wrong direction, who will never let you down. That One is Jesus Christ, God in the flesh. Doubters who are seekers will find Him.

Also check out: Humility, Inconsistency, Motives, Uncertainty, Worry, Zeal.

18

Drunkenness

"Woe to those who rise early in the morning that they may pursue strong drink; who stay up late in the evening that wine may inflame them! And their banquets are accompanied by lyre and harp, by tambourine and flute, and by wine; but they do not pay attention to the deeds of the Lord, nor do they consider the work of His hands" (Isaiah 5:11-12).

Susy is sixteen and the oldest child in the Markley family. Her dad's an elder in their church. Last Friday night, she was asked by the police to leave the football stands. The reason? She was drunk.

Chip and Stan are brothers. They attend Sunday school every week of the year. Chip has a five-year attendance pin. They were recently arrested in front of the high school late one night with several other boys. The charge? Public intoxication.

Laurie was caught stealing a stereo out of the Logans' home. But she wasn't responsible for her actions, she claimed. She was drunk.

You might fool your grandmother or deceive your parents about it, but it's a common fact: There's a lot of teenage drinking in our country. Many exhaustive reports pass around high school counselors' offices. Perhaps you've read some. But instead of looking at a pile of statistics, let's take a common-sense approach.

Getting drunk doesn't make sense because it doesn't produce happiness. Some people cry when they're drunk. Others fight. Drunkenness has never led to the good life for anyone. No matter how smoothly the television commercials glamorize it, I've never heard anyone give a testimony about the wonderful changes drunkenness had made in his life.

Drunkenness is bad for the body. Oscar knows. Oscar is dying at the age of fifty-eight because his insides are eaten up. "I can handle it," used to be his motto. But his body couldn't.

Drunkenness is bad for the health of others. A man beats his wife. A teen crashes head-on into a loaded school bus. An old man falls asleep in a flophouse and eleven people die in the fire caused by his unextinguished cigarette. All because someone was drunk.

Drunkenness is dumb because you willingly forfeit control over yourself. Think about it. What's so frightening about the thought of being buried alive? You would have no power to save yourself. Or why are we afraid of falling off a high cliff or tall building? Again, we fear loss of control. So why is it that people don't mind getting drunk? It just doesn't make sense.

Most important of all, drunkenness means zero value to the Lord's work in the world. One who is drunk can't think straight or act quickly or clearly. That's what the passage in Isaiah is saying. Who would want to pay that steep a price?

Fail to see what He's doing? Not me. I'm not about to miss out on any of the excitement.

Also check out: Boredom, Compromise, Depression, Failure, Frustration, Inferiority, Peer Pressure, Restitution, Self-control.

19

Failure

"But Peter said, 'Man, I do not know what you are talking about.' And immediately, while he was still speaking, a cock crowed. And the Lord turned and looked at Peter. And Peter remembered the word of the Lord, how He had told him, 'Before a cock crows today, you will deny Me three times.' And he went out and wept bitterly" (Luke 22:60-62).

"Mom, you'll never have to worry about me." Annette had just returned from having a physical exam. "Dr. Pierson suggested I get a prescription for birth control pills 'just in case.' I told him I wasn't that kind, that I was a Christian."

Annette's mom smiled and hugged her daughter. She was proud of Annette and enjoyed this moment of intimacy.

But just one year later, a white-faced Annette choked out the news. "Mom, Rick and I are going to get married in a few weeks. I'm pregnant."

Failure is a form of betrayal, the sense that you were unable to complete your own or someone else's expectations of what you are capable of doing. Peter knew what it meant to fail. So did Annette.

Judas was a failure, too. He realized his failure at about the same time as Peter did his. Judas the betrayer; Peter the denyer—both were failures. But the two men reacted in opposite ways.

Peter kept going. He faced himself squarely and accepted the truth about himself. When Jesus offered His forgiveness and acceptance again, Peter gladly took it. Peter the denyer became Peter the rock. And he was privileged to be used to convert over 3,000 people on Pentecost Day.

What about Judas? He gave up. His pride wouldn't allow him to confess and repent of his betrayal. He killed himself instead.

No one is immune to failure. But there isn't anyone who couldn't use failure as a steppingstone to some future success. New goals can be reached. A humble sense of our need for God's help could be admitted.

Annette had to work through her guilt and shame. She felt the burden of having disappointed her family and friends. But she set new goals for her life, goals that now included a husband and child. She made a renewed commitment to a daily walk with Christ.

After Rick finished his schooling and began to farm with his father and uncle, Annette completed high school during night classes. She graduated from a nursing course two years later.

Failure doesn't have to be a final verdict. God always has other alternatives to offer. He's been in this kind of business for a long, long time.

Also check out: Bitterness, Competition, Depression, Forgiveness, Frustration, Future, Grades, Guilt, Inferiority,

Pride, Self-worth, Shyness, Success, Trials, Victory. You might also want to read the book Failure: The Back Door to Success, *by Erwin Lutzer, Moody Press.*

20

Family

"Behold, how good and how pleasant it is for brothers to dwell together in unity! It is like the precious oil upon the head, coming down upon the beard, even Aaron's beard, coming down upon the edge of his robes. It is like the dew of Hermon, coming down upon the mountains of Zion; for there the Lord commanded the blessing—life forever" (Psalm 133:1-3).

How easy it is to say you love a starving child way off in famine-stricken India. But how hard it is to treat with consideration and kindness the one who shares your meals.

God knew it would be that way. He knew how we human beings are blind to our own weaknesses and needs. That's why He initiated the idea of family. The family is God's training ground for individuals to learn the lessons necessary for entering His eternal kingdom. It's also the boot camp for any useful ministry while we're still here on earth.

The divine family-unit plan provides every human being at least one place on this planet where he or she can be accepted and loved because "you're one of us." There's a place everyone can call home, a place to talk things out when you're hurting, a place to share joys when you win.

That was the original intention. But it hasn't always worked out that way.

There is hardly anyone in our present society who hasn't been pained either directly or indirectly by the tragedy of broken families. Even Christian families seem more prone than ever to neglect their unique role, and they are competing for a close second in the national statistics on broken families. Does that mean we might as well give up? Is there no use in trying anymore? We say a big "No!" Let's not give up. Ever.

No matter who you are or what kind of family situation you live in, there's something you can do to begin to build toward that divine plan: a kind word here; a listening ear there; a forgiving heart; an understanding shoulder to cry on.

Your family building plan might include reestablishing communication with a brother or a sister, a mother or a father. Maybe you don't have any blood relatives to build a family around. Ask God to show you those around you who could join with you in making a caring community.

Gary Sorenson was an illegitimate child. That's what one of his foster families told him. Anyway, his biological mother and father had abandoned him to society to find his own place to belong. The problem was that Gary also had a birth defect.

A severe cleft palate had left Gary with a scarred mouth and slurred speech, even after careful surgery. Since he wasn't an attractive baby or youngster, no one came forward to adopt him. So he just drifted from one foster family to another.

When Gary was a senior in high school, he met Nan Raney. Nan and Gary dated several times, and then Nan invited him to meet her family. Gary was very impressed. He made a firm decision soon after that first get-together. He was going to provide that kind of loving, caring family for his own kids some day.

Gary and Nan married during their senior year in college. But they found out after several miscarriages that Nan wouldn't be able to have children. That's when they began to open their home to rejects, kids such as Gary had been. The Sorensons now have six children. One has cerebral palsy. Another has a heart problem. The twins are chronic diabetics. One is blind. The youngest is deaf. But they each have a precious gift—a stable, caring home.

Gary determined early in his life not to allow his pitiful upbringing to lead into another generation of despair. He did what he could to break the chain of what could have become a vicious cycle.

God's plan for family doesn't always mean marriage. God calls males and females to the single life, too. But that doesn't exclude the call to reach out, to care, to build bridges within the community all around you. Single people still need someone close enough to rub them wrong when they need a growing spell and to stand by them when they get into trouble. That's what family is all about.

Also check out: Dating, Friends, Love, Marriage, Purpose, Selfishness, Trials.

21

Fear

"And I say to you, My friends, do not be afraid of those who kill the body, and after that have no more that they can do. But I will warn you whom to fear: fear the One who after He has killed has authority to cast into hell; yes, I tell you, fear Him! Are not five sparrows sold for two cents? And yet not one of them is forgotten before God. Indeed, the very hairs of your head are all numbered. Do not fear; you are of more value than many sparrows" (Luke 12:4-7).

Our family was camping in the Cascades of California, near Mount Lassen. A thunderstorm blew in suddenly while we cleared the dinner dishes. Our son Russell pulled out his watch with a second hand and began counting the time between lightning flash and thunder roll. "Four miles away," he announced. "Three miles away," "two miles away," and then—*crash!* A powerful bolt slammed into a giant tree less than fifty feet from where we stood.

I trembled as we watched a wide strip of smoking bark peel from the top to the bottom of that majestic redwood. I had never been that close to lightning before. It shook me so much that I felt paralyzed to the spot. I didn't feel alert to my old self again until Russell and his younger brother, Mike, darted over to the stripped tree. Concern for their safety snapped me out of my self-concern.

There are many kinds of fear, and there is a wide variety of things in this world to be afraid of. At times our walk on earth can feel like a daring game of Russian Roulette. Even popes, presidents, and pop singers aren't exempt from the violent possibilities.

But nearly every one of our fears centers on one main fear: the fear of death. One of the reasons Jesus Christ came was to free us from that fear. He knew that when we cease to fear death, we won't fear life, either. Then we can boldly complete our appointed tasks and leave the end results to our heavenly Father.

However, fear can be healthy, too. Just the right dose can keep us out of dangerous situations. The highest fear of all, that reverential awe that God deserves, can lead a person to spiritual life and away from the dreadful consequences of God's just wrath.

Bob Krone was registered alone in the Liberty Hotel. His high school graduating class had spent the day at a nearby recreation park that featured concerts, rides, and a play. All his classmates had returned home on the bus. But Bob planned to stay the weekend with his father, who would be picking him up the next morning.

With a fresh pepperoni and cheese pizza and a large cola, Bob settled back in an easy chair to watch an old movie on TV. He must have fallen asleep sometime before the movie ended, because the next thing he knew, he awoke with a start to find the TV screen all fuzzy and smoke billowing under the crack of the door. He jumped up and opened the door. Smoke and searing heat greeted him.

He ran to the bathroom and plunged a towel under the

faucet, then stuffed it at the bottom of the door. He raced to the window and watched a fire truck just pull in. He was six floors up. Bob frantically tried to think of what the best action would be. Should he chance running down the hall? Should he wrap himself in wet sheets? Should he prepare for a possible jump?

Bob experienced his first taste of sheer terror. Most of all, he didn't want to die, especially not this way. As the stifling heat of the walls pressed in around him, he cried out to God. A quiet, relaxing peace filled him.

Bob Krone was a Christian. During that moment of peace, he recalled the assurance he had that even if this was his time to die, he could enter God's presence with a clear conscience. His public confession of Christ as his Savior and daily walk with Him were his assurance. He wasn't afraid anymore.

A few minutes later, a hotel staff person brought him an oxygen mask and led him to a fire escape. From that night on, Bob began to really live. He boldly witnessed to several of the fire victims and his own dad for the first time. He's had many opportunities since then to tell what he learned during that crisis about a fear that was faced and conquered, and about the God who made it possible.

Also check out: Boldness, Death, Purpose, Trauma, Victory, Violence, Worry, Zeal.

*Forgiveness- To pardon or give up Resent-
ment, when someone has wronged us. To
give up the right to get even.*

22

Forgiveness

*"Then Peter came and said to Him, 'Lord, how often shall
my brother sin against me and I forgive him? Up to seven
times?' Jesus said to him, 'I do not say to you, up to seven
times, but up to seventy times seven'" (Matthew 18:21-22).*

Have you ever stopped to wonder why God bothers to
forgive any of us? The continual need to forgive millions of
rebellious, obnoxious human beings must be tiresome,
even to God. But the Bible gives us some clues about why
God forgives.

He forgives because He truly feels compassion for us
when we get ourselves into messes. He cares when we hurt
ourselves and the people around us. He enjoys bringing us
the relief of a new start, another opportunity to find His
good and perfect will.

Our God forgives because it's important for us to admit
how small and helpless we are without Him. To think too
highly of who and what we are gets us nowhere. When we
humbly kneel in worship before Him, He is able and willing
to exalt us to a place of honor of His choosing.

God has a plan for human history. He also has a plan for
each individual that somehow fits in with the larger plan. If
God never forgave, His plan would never work. No one
would be left to be blessed by it or to fulfill it.

The greatest sin of all is to decline that costly but freely offered forgiveness. Pride does that, as do such attitudes as bitterness, anger, jealousy, and the like. Each of those ugly, inner turmoils has to do with our relationships with people.

Think of God's forgiveness of us relative to the forgiveness He asks us to offer others. It's like comparing a gift worth $10 million to a gift of eighteen cents. God offers us a $10 million forgiveness, and all He asks is that we give up our eighteen cents worth of forgiving to those few who do us wrong. Even the worst math student could figure that one out. We've got the best end of the deal.

To forgive is a promise not to bring the matter up anymore—not to the one who hurt you, not to anyone else, not even to yourself.

What about consequences? some ask. Does that mean anyone can go out and do whatever he wants and then ask for forgiveness and the slate's clean?

First of all, we can't fool God. He knows a lying heart when He sees one. Either we are sorry for what we've done or we're not. A person who truly grieves over his wrongs isn't going to turn right around and commit the same sin again.

Second, yes, the slate is wiped clean. But often there are still penalties to pay.

Moses misused God's power in a fit of anger. He was forgiven, but he wasn't allowed to enter the Promised Land.

David committed adultery with Bathsheba. He was forgiven, but his baby son died and his family faced many turmoils in the years that followed.

Some consequences are just the irreversible results of

situations that can't be undone. A murderer can't bring back his victim. A wasted year can't be lived over. A harsh word can't be taken back.

"Forgive!" our Lord commands. If He commands it, it must be within our Spirit-infused will's power to accomplish. It's not easy, but it's not impossible.

Also check out: Anger, Bitterness, Criticism, Greed, Humility, Jealousy, Pettiness, Pride, Restitution, Ungratefulness.

23

Friends

"Now it came about when he had finished speaking to Saul, that the soul of Jonathan was knit to the soul of David, and Jonathan loved him as himself. . . . Then Jonathan made a covenant with David because he loved him as himself. And Jonathan stripped himself of the robe that was on him and gave it to David, with his armor, including his sword and his bow and his belt" (1 Samuel 18:1, 3-4).

There are some things that can't be done alone. It is almost impossible, all by yourself, to play tennis, get your yearbook autographed, see food caught in your tooth, find that rip in the back of your pants, talk on the phone, cruise Main Street, or eat a whole giant sundae at the local ice cream parlor. God made us to be dependent social beings. Oh, I know, there are those who claim they don't need anybody, that they are content just taking care of themselves and letting the rest of the world slip by. But the fact remains that the give-and-take interaction between fellow human beings is the quickest route to becoming whole, well-rounded personalities.

We all need one or two trusted friends whom we feel close enough to that we can talk over all the crazy notions in our minds and hear them say, "Hey, that really is crazy," or "I

know what you mean; I've gone through the same thing."
Our tumbling thoughts need to be sorted out sometimes by
another person's more-or-less objective point of view.

But friends like that aren't easy to find. Trust and
comfortable companionship take time to build. And the
saying still holds true: "If you want a good friend, first, you
need to learn how to *be* a good friend."

Do you want a friend who knows when to keep a secret?
Then don't gossip. Do you want a friend who's interested in
the things you're good at doing? Then be willing to try new
activities and explore new subjects. Do you like being
around attractive people but don't want them stealing your
dates? Then take care of yourself and don't be a flirt.

David and Jonathan had a unique bond. Their friendship
lasted through some tough times and trials. When Jonathan
was killed, David kept his promise for the rest of his life to
do what he could for Jonathan's surviving family. To be a true
friend can cost you something. Ask yourself, "What can I
give to this two-way relationship?"

Then there is the friend who sticks closer than a brother.
While you're in the pursuit of making and keeping friends,
don't forget Jesus Christ. A human friend will always have
certain limitations. Even the closest buddy can disappoint
you at times. But not Jesus. You can tell Him anything,
because He already knows everything. He can give you
advice and help in any kind of situation. He's the perfect
kind of friend.

But getting to know Jesus that well will take time and
effort. Just as with a human relationship, knowledge of God
and His Son doesn't come automatically. Do you know what

He likes? What He dislikes? Do you know how He spends His time? Do you know what things are important to Him? How much time each day, each week do you spend with Him? To know God as a personal friend—is there a privilege any higher?

Also check out: Bitterness, Boredom, Bragging, Clothes, Competition, Compromise, Criticism, Depression, Forgiveness, Jealousy, Peer Pressure, Restitution, Self-worth, Shyness.

24

Frustration

"And they passed through the Phrygian and Galatian region, having been forbidden by the Holy Spirit to speak the word in Asia; and when they had come to Mysia, they were trying to go into Bithynia, and the Spirit of Jesus did not permit them; and passing by Mysia, they came down to Troas. And a vision appeared to Paul in the night: a certain man of Macedonia was standing and appealing to him, and saying, 'Come over to Macedonia and help us.' And when he had seen the vision, immediately we sought to go into Macedonia, concluding that God had called us to preach the gospel to them" (Acts 16:6-10).

Ever since he was six years old, Bret has wanted to be a mechanic. He worked for hours on his tricycle, his bike, his motorcycle, and then his car. When he graduated from high school, there was no doubt where he would go. Lewis-Clark State College offered the finest mechanics program in the state. That's why Bret applied in November of his senior year.

In March he was notified that he had been accepted. The last week of August he paid his fees, reserved a dorm room, and waited for final registration.

That's when he got another note. "We're very sorry, but

99

there has been a mixup. We're over-registered in this program, and you'll have to wait for an opening."

Bret couldn't believe it. He'd quit his summer job, paid over $1,500, and now they were telling him they were all booked up. It was too late to change schools. The only alternative was sitting through a whole semester or more of general education classes, the very thing he hadn't wanted to do. Bret was frustrated.

Frustration is the feeling of being prevented from achieving what you set out to accomplish. We all experience it one way or another. Look at the apostle Paul and his companions.

Paul had a big idea for ministry in a part of Asia we now call southern Russia. Along the way he and his helpers planned to preach in every town and village they entered. But the goal couldn't be reached. Once they arrived in Asia, they were forbidden to speak at all. We have no idea just how the Holy Spirit prevented their speaking. Perhaps it was a physical ailment or a government censure.

Finally they reached the borders of southern Russia. However, again the Holy Spirit wouldn't let them enter. Borders closed. What a great time they were having. They left home telling everyone about the great things they'd accomplish, and now they had nothing to report.

But all was not lost. As they sat around in Troas, God spoke to Paul in a vision. The gospel was to go to Europe for the first time, and they were to be His channels. They quickly responded. When the dust settled on Paul's adventures, the trip had proved to be a turning point in Christian history. The good news spread across all of Europe, and from there to the ends of the earth.

How about the frustrations in your life? How do you handle them? Here are some helpful hints to consider.

1. Your whole life is in God's hands. Desire His will above your own.

2. Frustration hurts. Don't take it lightly. But remember, obstacles don't necessarily mean the end of an idea.

3. See delay as a pause in the action, a time to reevaluate your direction.

4. Are you trying a short cut? Perhaps you need to back up and do the job more carefully.

5. Are you headed in the wrong direction? Maybe the project should be abandoned.

6. An obstacle may be a test of your determination. Are you sure this is what you really want?

7. Try again. Don't let one problem sidetrack a worthy goal.

Bret sat through a series of boring lectures until January. He was assured of a place in mechanics school. Was that whole semester wasted? Not really. You see, in the English class he met Carrie. They're engaged now.

Also check out: Anger, Boldness, Competition, Depression, Failure, Future, Grades, Greed, Purpose, Success, Victory, Vocation, Zeal.

25

Future

"Come now, you who say, 'Today or tomorrow, we shall go to such and such a city, and spend a year there and engage in business and make a profit.' Yet you do not know what your life will be like tomorrow. You are just a vapor that appears for a little while and then vanishes away. Instead, you ought to say, 'If the Lord wills, we shall live and also do this or that'" (James 4:13-15).

Some people wish their whole life was figured out. But I wonder if they'd really be happy knowing what will be in their futures. Consider Annamarie.

At seventeen, Annamarie is dying of curiosity to know whom she'll marry. She has even prayed that God would show her the one. But nothing's happened yet. She sighs about it a lot. *If I only knew,* she thinks, *I could make concrete plans about what to do with my life. If I'm going to marry a doctor, I should take a nursing course. If he'll be a professional athlete, I'll need to study investment counseling. But if he's going to be a millionaire, ah, then I won't have to prepare for anything at all except how to recover from jet lag.*

There are some things we're better off not knowing. Timing is important. Knowing too much beforehand is like opening a Christmas present before Christmas. The anticipation fizzles.

The Bible offers us some common-sense suggestions for handling worries about the future.

First, *plan.* That's right, God wants you to plan. Jesus planned His route to the other side of the lake. Paul plotted out his missionary journeys. A Christian should make plans. What do you want to be doing one month from now? One year from now? How about five years from now?

Second, *commit your plans to God.* The final decision is always His. Check out your ideas with His Word. Would there be any objections there? Make the Lord an active partner in your future goals.

Third, *work hard to complete your plans.* Don't sit back and do nothing. In the James passage at the beginning of this devotional, the instructions given are to go ahead with business deals, but always with the disclaimer at the root of your attitudes, "If the Lord wills, we will do this or that."

The Lord God can be trusted with the future. After all, He's the One who

- created everything in heaven and on earth (Colossians 1:16).
- holds the world together (Colossians 1:17).
- supplies every good gift (James 1:17).
- does all things well (Mark 7:37).
- knows everything about you (Psalm 139:16).
- is the beginning and the end (Revelation 1:8).
- has all authority (Matthew 28:18).
- now lives in the future and is busy preparing a place for you when you arrive (John 14:1-3).

Also check out: Boldness, Dating, Family, Fear, Marriage, Purpose, Success, Victory, Vocation, Worry.

26

Grades

"Then after an interval of fourteen years I went up again to Jerusalem with Barnabas, taking Titus along also. And it was because of a revelation that I went up; and I submitted to them the gospel which I preach among the Gentiles, but I did so in private to those who were of reputation, for fear that I might be running, or had run, in vain" (Galatians 2:1-2).

Honor Roll. Dean's List. Summa Cum Laude. Straight A's. Four-point average. Those are the proud achievements that many students strive for.

Glenn felt the pressure. His grades were down again. Another deficiency note was in the mail. He could feel it coming. Dad would get mad, Mom would be disappointed, and his sister would make some snide remark. But Glenn had his defense ready this time. He was prepared the day the letter from the principal's office arrived.

"Dad," he began, "it's like this. I get good grades on my tests. It's just that I don't get all my homework turned in. Doing those assignments is a waste of time. And about the book report, I turned that in late because of going to church winter camp. As you can see, the whole system's unfair since I do well on the tests."

Glenn's dad wasn't impressed. While Glenn thought

school would be much better without grades, his dad was thinking school would be much better if Glenn didn't keep getting deficiency notes.

Grades perform a useful function. They can be a measurement of just how much you're learning. They can give you a progress report on where you stand in the educational process. We measure our height by using a tape. We try to measure the mind's efforts by grading.

Grades are also a tool for teachers to use to analyze their teaching. Few teachers enjoy flunking students. It's a failure for them as well as for the student. They weren't able to help this one learn.

Grades can also give students an honest look at themselves, at the kinds of students they are.

Paul didn't mind having his doctrine inspected by the church at Jerusalem. He was concerned enough to want to know if he was on the right track. Someone who considers himself an *A* student but always gets *C*'s had better reexamine his study habits.

Finally, grades aren't the most important thing in life. Good and perfect grades won't insure a future of success, happiness, or wealth. And poor grades have never doomed anyone to a life of failure. Grades are only one road sign along the path of maturity.

Also check out: Competition, Depression, Failure, Frustration, Future, Happiness, Purpose, Self-worth, Self-control, Success, Vocation.

27

Greed

"But a certain man named Ananias, with his wife Sapphira, sold a piece of property, and kept back some of the price for himself, with his wife's full knowledge, and bringing a portion of it, he laid it at the apostles' feet. But Peter said, 'Ananias, why has Satan filled your heart to lie to the Holy Spirit, and to keep back some of the price of the land? While it remained unsold, did it not remain your own? And after it was sold, was it not under your control? Why is it that you have conceived this deed in your heart? You have not lied to men, but to God'" (Acts 5:1-4).

"I want it! I want it! I want it!" That's the way little kids act. But we all outgrow that stage—don't we?

Todd hates for his brother, Tedd, to dish up the ice cream. Tedd always grabs the biggest bowl for himself.

Lori is furious with Anna. "How dare she buy that yellow dress down in Mason's window!" Lori said. "She heard me say I wanted it." But Lori didn't want to spend "her" money, so she had been trying to talk her mother into buying it for her. Meanwhile, Anna thought Lori had lost interest.

Clayton had the two best lockers in the gym. That gave him more room for his football pads. Meanwhile, another player had to use a locker at the other end of the gym. But so what? "He's just a freshman," Clayton said.

Greed is ugly. It's the unreasonable desire to acquire more than you need, and it often leads to a fixation of the mind on that object you want. Greed is the expression of a mind that thinks only of itself. I want more ice cream. I want a yellow dress. I want two lockers. Greed makes the statement, "I am the most important person here, and everyone else had better react accordingly."

Most of all, greed is a direct affront to God, because it implies that He is incapable of providing His children with the abundant life He promised. Scheming, deceiving, and cheating are the end results of a heart full of greed.

Ananias and Sapphira got caught in the greed trap. They looked with envy at the honor others were receiving because of the sacrificial sums of money they gave to the church. They wanted some of that glory, so they sold their property. Then suddenly the sum seemed bigger than they had first thought. They hesitated and finally decided to keep some back for themselves but pretend they had given it all to the church.

Ananias and Sapphira didn't have to give it all. Giving to God is always voluntary. But they lied about it in order to gain prestige. They didn't count on the Holy Spirit's revealing their lie to Peter. He confronted them and they both dropped dead. That was quite an object lesson.

Greed has a price. It sucks the life out of your soul and spirit. Whenever greed is a temptation to you, consider these questions:

Can I get by without having this for another six months?

Will I be depriving someone else?

Will having this give me increased honor and status?

Can I be content if someone else receives this instead?
Will I have to do some maneuvering to get this, or can I
wait for God to provide this for me in His way, in His time?

*Also check out: Clothes, Frustration, Jealousy, Materialism,
Selfishness, Ungratefulness.*

28

Griping

"Do all things without grumbling or disputing; that you may prove yourselves to be blameless and innocent, children of God above reproach in the midst of a crooked and perverse generation, among whom you appear as lights in the world, holding fast the word of life, so that in the day of Christ I may have cause to glory because I did not run in vain nor toil in vain" (Philippians 2:14-16).

Are you a griper? If you made a record of a typical day's conversations and thoughts, what would it look like? Would it look something like this?

6:30 A.M. "Leave me alone! I'm just too tired to get up."

7:00 A.M. "Mother, he's taking too long in the shower."

7:30 A.M. "You *know* I don't like runny eggs."

8:00 A.M. "You little kids ought to sit three in a seat so there's more room for us."

8:30 A.M. "What do you mean, sick? She promised to bring my English book today."

9:00 A.M. "This must be the worst substitute teacher in the county."

10:00 A.M. "A surprise quiz? It just isn't *fair!*"

11:00 A.M. "Why does Darren always look at that blonde in that way?"

12:00 noon	"I'm not going to eat next to her again."
1:00 P.M.	"But you've already called on me twice this week."
2:00 P.M.	"Well, that's easy for you to say. Your hair isn't thin and wispy like mine."
3:00 P.M.	"You call this a car?"
4:00 P.M.	"Roger opened my mail!"
5:00 P.M.	"Ruthie never had to cook dinner."
6:00 P.M.	"Do I *have* to go to Bible study tonight?"
6:01 P.M.	"But I don't have anything to wear."
7:00 P.M.	"I hate sitting in the front."
8:00 P.M.	"But mother, I wanted to stay and talk with Tony."
9:00 P.M.	"But I can't do my homework without the stereo on."
10:00 P.M.	"You treat me like a kid. It's only ten."

The funny thing about griping is that it can become a way of life and the griper doesn't even realize it. The people around him do, of course. But griping seldom if ever accomplishes its intended purpose, especially the more we use it. Very few people or situations change because of a gripe. So, why do we gripe? The spirit and impact of most complaints just increase the very irritation we're trying to eliminate.

And there are many other things griping does not do for us. It does not increase our satisfaction or happiness. It does not build up our popularity standing. It does not produce a positive response in other people. It doesn't promote dignity and self-worth. It doesn't create an atmosphere of love and fairness.

To gripe is to waste time and effort. It's the common way of people, however. That's what you should expect from lost and sinful humanity. But what about Christians? Paul says we have an opportunity to really shine out as a different breed and prove we're children of God. How? By doing "all things without grumbling or disputing."

Can you imagine what it would be like to be around people who never gripe or to be a person who never whines? What would your family say? What would your friends think? What would your teachers do? Finally, what would your heavenly Father think?

Also check out: Anger, Criticism, Disobedience, Friends, Frustration, Happiness, Humility, Pettiness, Ungratefulness.

29

Guilt

"For if the blood of goats and bulls and the ashes of a heifer sprinkling those who have been defiled, sanctify for the cleansing of the flesh, how much more will the blood of Christ, who through the eternal Spirit offered Himself without blemish to God, cleanse your conscience from dead works to serve the living God?" (Hebrews 9:13-14).

For weeks Valerie relived the whole sequence of events. The excitement of the senior Christmas party had been building all fall. The entertainment began at the high school gym, and then all the couples would eat at a fancy restaurant right on the end of the pier, overlooking the ocean. She paired off with Taylor, of course. They had been dating for almost a year.

The party was great. The dinner afterward at The Lobster Tale was good. Everyone ordered the works. Taylor never looked so handsome. *He could be a movie star someday,* Valerie had thought.

After dinner was the slow drive home. Valerie hated for the magical night to end. "I wish we didn't have to get right home," Valerie finally said.

"Well, we could stop off by Creek's Park and talk some."

"Sure, why not?" she had answered.

Dumb. Dumb. Dumb. Valerie grimaced as she remembered. *Why didn't I think up something else to do?*

But Valerie felt so mature that night. She thought she could handle any situation. They talked. That led to a hug and a kiss. ~~Usually that's all that happened. But the kissing went on and on until~~—*Oh, no, not us,* Valerie thought, groaning inwardly.

Taylor felt bad about it, too. He couldn't even bring himself to call her for several days. That compounded Valerie's depression. What did he think of her? Was their friendship over? What would happen from there?

Guilt can be a good thing. It shows that you have standards and values that you attempt to live by. You are a person of principle. To have no guilt at all is sad. But guilt should be a motivation for the following action:

Confess. Admit to God what He already knows. You blew it. You failed. This was not just a mere prick in your conscience, but a sin against Him. Agree with Him that it was wrong and that you need His forgiveness.

Apologize. Make the situation right with others who have been wronged. Let them know you care about your influence on their lives. They're important to you.

Rededicate. Renew your promise to yourself not to do that anymore. So you messed up. That means starting at square one, but it doesn't mean you can't have another chance.

Guilt should so humble us that we're more sensitive to the struggles with temptation of those around us. Be slow to condemn, quick to encourage. We need to help one another through the many trials of living. Few can make it alone.

Allow God to cleanse away all your guilt. That's why He

sent Jesus, to provide a way out when we fall down. Otherwise, none of us would ever make it.

Valerie did a stupid thing. It was more than stupid. It was sin. But she did not commit the unforgivable sin. With a cleared conscience and a right relationship with her loving, heavenly Father, she and Taylor can still work to build self-control.

Also check out: Compromise, Dating, Disobedience, Drunkenness, Failure, Forgiveness, Humility, Love, Purpose, Restitution, Self-control, Sexuality.

30

Happiness

"You call Me Teacher and Lord; and you are right; for so I am. If I then, the Lord and the Teacher, washed your feet, you also ought to wash one another's feet. For I gave you an example that you also should do as I did to you. Truly, truly, I say to you, a slave is not greater than his master; neither one who is sent greater than the one who sent him. If you know these things, you are blessed if you do them" (John 13:13-17).

Jerry knew exactly what would make him happy: a Datsun 280ZX. He decided on his sixteenth birthday to find a way to get one. He found a job on the weekends at Paula's Pizza Parlour. After school he pumped gas at Thompson's. He didn't attend any football games, school socials, or weekend camping trips. He had a goal, and he was determined to reach it. By this time next year, he would pay cash for a brand new car with all the extras.

Jerry's grades and social life began to suffer. But Jerry worked on. He even put in hours on Sundays and holidays. Then the great and glorious day finally arrived. How proud he was to pull up to the pizza parlour in that sporty, new car.

But Jerry is still working as hard as ever. He's got gas and upkeep and repairs to pay for. He didn't realize what an expense a foreign car could be. And there's also the insurance.

Some of his old baseball buddies came by Paula's the other day for an after-game snack. "Hey, Jerry," they shouted, "must be something driving that thing around. You must be the happiest guy in town." Then they piled into Peter's broken-down Ford as they laughed and shouted about a hilarious double play.

On nights like that, Jerry finds it hard to sleep. He keeps wondering if it's been worth it.

Happiness is so elusive. To be really happy, you must be content with your position, your condition, and your worth to God and the people around you. Joy often dominates a life like that. But that can be a quiet kind of joy as well as the super-bubble-over type. The Bible tells us that happiness is a state of blessedness. To be blessed and to be happy are the same thing.

Jesus said He came, among other reasons, to be an example for us. He showed us how to relate to God and how to treat people. He knew how much all of us want to be happy. That's why He told us,

"Blessed are the poor in spirit. . . . "

"Blessed are those who mourn. . . . "

"Blessed are the gentle. . . . "

"Blessed are those who hunger and thirst for righteousness. . . . "

"Blessed are the merciful. . . . "

"Blessed are the pure in heart. . . . "

"Blessed are the peacemakers. . . . "

Matthew 5:3-9

Happiness is a two-way street. You must make your peace with God. You must give of yourself to help other people. Any other pursuit leads down a dead end. If you don't believe me, ask Jerry.

Also check out: Apathy, Boredom, Depression, Failure, Future, Materialism, Purpose, Self-worth, Success, Victory, Worry.

31

Humility

"And they came to John, and said to him, 'Rabbi, He who was with you beyond the Jordan, to whom you have borne witness, behold, He is baptizing, and all are coming to Him.' John answered and said, 'A man can receive nothing, unless it has been given him from heaven. You yourselves bear me witness, that I said, "I am not the Christ," but, "I have been sent before Him." He who has the bride is the bridegroom; but the friend of the bridegroom, who stands and hears him, rejoices greatly because of the bridegroom's voice. And so this joy of mine has been made full. He must increase, but I must decrease'" (John 3:26-30).

The crowd began to clap and cheer as Marti entered the auditorium. Soon Mr. Markes made the formal announcement that everybody already knew: Marti was the new homecoming queen. When Mr. Markes handed Marti the microphone, she said, "I really don't deserve this honor." Marti didn't really believe that, nor did anyone else. It just sounded like the right thing to say.

Marti had spent months and years preparing for this event. That's why she ran for freshman class cheerleader. That's why she agreed to be chairman of the sophomore Jog-A-Thon. That's why she talked her parents into sponsoring the steak barbecue for their league-champion football team. That's why she liked to be friendly with just about everybody in the whole school. You had better believe Marti deserved it. But that's all right. Who would want a humble homecoming queen?

We have a knack for twisting good and bad character traits. Take humility, for instance. Most people would consider that a weakness rather than a strength. "It's OK to be humble—when you can't be anything else."

True humility is knowing who you are and who you aren't while truly caring more about what happens to the other guy. Few people have it. But John the Baptist did.

Just as John's ministry was going full steam, some of his followers began to desert him. They wanted to go hear the new prophet in town, the one called Jesus. How fickle and ungrateful could they be? John had dedicated his life to unselfish sacrifice. No family. No nice home. No feasts and parties. Just simple living and faithfulness in speaking God's message. Now what did it get him? Most of us would call it a stab in the back by his own friends.

That's not the way John the Baptist saw the situation, however. He claimed that it brought him great joy. Then he made this statement: "He must increase, but I must decrease." That could be a definition for humility. John's purpose was to increase the status, popularity, and position of Jesus, not his own. What is your purpose?

Does history record John as a weak man? It certainly does not. Did he waste his potential and just sit around acting humble? Not at all. John the Baptist knew who he was and who he wasn't. He knew what God wanted him to do, and he got up the courage to do it—nothing more, nothing less. Later Jesus would say of him: "Truly, I say to you, among those born of women there has not arisen anyone greater than John the Baptist" (Matthew 11:11a).

The greatest man on earth was humble, obedient John.

Also check out: Anger, Apathy, Bragging, Competition, Criticism, Jealousy, Lying, Motives, Pride, Shyness.

32

Illness

"And because of the surpassing greatness of the revelations, for this reason, to keep me from exalting myself, there was given me a thorn in the flesh, a messenger of Satan to buffet me—to keep me from exalting myself! Concerning this I entreated the Lord three times that it might depart from me. And He has said to me, 'My grace is sufficient for you, for power is perfected in weakness.' Most gladly, therefore, I will rather boast about my weaknesses, that the power of Christ may dwell in me. Therefore I am well content with weaknesses, with insults, with distresses, with persecutions, with difficulties, for Christ's sake; for when I am weak, then I am strong" (2 Corinthians 12:7-10).

Asthma. The dictionary defines this condition as a weakness in the lungs characterized by decreases in the diameter of some air passages.

Allen slammed the book shut. "Ha! That's just a fancy way to say I can't play baseball, I can't play football, and I can't even chase my dog without severe cramps."

Allen's mother suggested to him that his asthma was a thorn in the flesh that God allowed to exist for some special purpose.

127

"I don't want to hear it," he had shouted. Now he wondered to himself, *What kind of God would want a guy to hurt so much?*

That's a question asked by many victims of disease and handicaps, and by their loved ones. Why does God allow such misery to continue?

God created a perfect world. Adam and Eve were perfect specimens of health, and their environment was disaster-free. Then they chose to disobey God. That act of their will not only altered the course of their own lives, but their billions of descendants were affected, too. Human sin messed up a beautiful creation. All nature has been groaning and moaning ever since. Viruses, violence, volcanic eruptions, and earthquakes are just some of the results.

Our creator God wanted something better for us. But we chose our own way. Now we have to put up with the penalties. Still, He is sensitive to our every need. He cares about our aches and pains. Sometimes He relieves us. At other times he allows us to experience those discomforts for His high purpose. A postponed healing might mean a lesson to learn, a ministry to receive or give, or another hurting person with whom to empathize.

This principle is a part of practical living. A parent refuses to let a child eat a peanut-butter-and-jelly sandwich at 5:00 because he knows there will be turkey and gravy served at 5:30. But the child feels the blow. How could this otherwise loving parent deny a helpless kid a sandwich? He does it only when he wants something better for his children.

The hardest lesson a Christian can learn is to give God a chance to work out His plans. That may take time. It may mean His saying no for now. It may mean suffering a little while. Meanwhile, we are free to use every option of medical knowledge at our disposal to heal, comfort, and rehabilitate. Illness doesn't last forever, even if it's a lifetime ailment.

By the way, Allen still has his asthma. But he's stopped being bitter about it. He learned that jogging was the right medicine for him. Not only did that strengthen his lungs, but he has also competed in running events all over the state. He even won a few. Allen is elated to find something athletic that he can do, and he gives his best efforts to it.

Also check out: Bitterness, Competition, Depression, Family, Frustration, Humility, Inferiority, Purpose, Success, Trials, Ungratefulness, Zeal.

33

Inconsistency

"Again, you have heard that the ancients were told, 'You shall not make false vows, but shall fulfill your vows to the Lord.' But I say to you, make no oath at all, either by heaven, for it is the throne of God, or by the earth, for it is the footstool of His feet, or by Jerusalem, for it is the city of the great King. Nor shall you make an oath by your head, for you cannot make one hair white or black. But let your statement be, 'Yes, yes' or 'No, no'; and anything beyond these is of evil" (Matthew 5:33-37).

The code of the West used to be that a man was as good as his word. It's just not true anymore. Signed and sealed contracts are scoured for loopholes. Our courts are crammed with people trying to reverse previous commitments or actions.

Scott is an agreeable boy. It's just his nature. When his dad says, "Don't forget to take out the trash," he answers, "Sure, Dad." Mom reminds him to make his bed. "Be happy to," comes the reply. Sis asks if he'll drop off her book at the library. "No problem!" he says with a smile.

The only trouble is that the trash is still in the house; the bed is made by a disgruntled Mom; and his sister's book lies on the kitchen table. Scott's words don't mean much.

Jesus said to let your "yes" mean yes and your "no" mean no. Actions should match words. We need to think through

131

the promises we have made. Suppose you were asked to be a campaign manager for a friend who's running for class president. First, review what you would need to do. Would the responsibilities conflict with any present commitments? Figure that out before you decide to say, "Oh, sure, I'll do it."

No promise is too small to keep. Resist the temptation to consider your words to certain people or in minor (to you) situations to be of little importance. Practice being consistent in every matter that involves your word. If Mrs. Savage asks you to serve at the open house dinner and you agree, let nothing stand in your way.

When we delay acting on a commitment, we increase the chance that it will be neglected. If we quickly complete it, we can be free of the mental burden. "Why, I'm so swamped I don't know where to start" is the motto of one who is a tardy over-committer.

The following is a test of your dependability:

1. Do you (always) (usually) (sometimes) (never) complete an assigned task (immediately) (sooner or later) (by a given date) (when I'm forced to)?

2. Do you have to punctuate your answers with extra emphasis like, "Really, really, *really*, I'll do it"?

3. Are you saying "no" inside the whole time your mouth says "yes"?

4. Do you find it easy to find excuses for reneging on a commitment?

5. Would your friends call you unpredictable?

Also check out: Compromise, Friends, Lying, Motives, Purpose, Selfishness, Uncertainty, Zeal.

34

Inferiority ✳

"I urge you therefore, brethren, by the mercies of God, to present your bodies a living and holy sacrifice, acceptable to God, which is your spiritual service of worship. And do not be conformed to this world, but be transformed by the renewing of your mind, that you may prove what the will of God is, that which is good and acceptable and perfect. For through the grace given to me I say to every man among you not to think more highly of himself than he ought to think; but to think so as to have sound judgment, as God has allotted to each a measure of faith" (Romans 12:1-3).

Such a sickly child, no one expected him to amount to much. Always in the shadow of an older brother, he was known as the skinny kid. But he decided to change that image. He mustered up his courage and tried out for sports: soccer, swimming, and weight lifting. He made physical fitness goals for himself and then reached them one by one.

Now he has thirteen world championship records to his credit, including Mr. Olympia, Mr. World, and Mr. Universe. Arnold Schwarzenegger's name is synonymous with "pumping iron." No inferiority there.

But have you ever heard of Skip Procter, the one that lives in Three Forks, Montana? No? Well, it's no wonder. He's lucky to press his own weight, which is only 110 pounds.

Skip is the fifth son of J. J. and Martha Procter. The oldest, Todd, was quarterback on the Bobcat football team and student body president during his time in high school. Then comes Clint. He holds the record for most career tackles at State. Number three son, Travis, plays pro ball up in Alaska. Jake, a senior in high school, led his team to the all-league championship this year. And then there's Skip. J. J. jokes that when Skip turned out to be such a runt, they decided that was enough kids. Everyone laughs—everyone except Skip.

Lift weights? Run three miles? Eat spinach? You name it, he's tried it, and it was all no good. He still doesn't look or perform as a Procter should. Skip is miserable.

He's not alone. We all know someone in his same shape. But God doesn't make mistakes. Each of us has the size, shape, and mental capacity that He intended for us. We're not made of inferior materials; the arrangement's just uniquely different.

What we do with what God has given to us is important. We need to make the effort to discover what we can accomplish within our particular limitations. Laziness can produce inferior feelings.

Comparing ourselves to others is a lousy way to judge self-worth. Each individual is like an iceberg. You only see about 10 percent of what they really are. You can't even analyze their total physical makeup, much less do more than take a quick glimpse at their mental abilities or spiritual depth. To know another human being in all the minute details takes insight that only God has.

Do you have any idea what God expects of you? You can't know until you commit yourself to His Son as your Savior and Lord and take a good look at the Scriptures on a regular basis. Without that anchor, you could press 600 pounds and still not find satisfaction.

With God's help and guidance, dream some dreams. Set a reachable goal, then another and another. Watch for a life's message and purpose to develop as you experiment. There may be a surprise or two just around the corner if you'll get out there and look for it.

Also check out: Boldness, Competition, Depression, Failure, Frustration, Future, Grades, Purpose, Self-worth, Shyness, Success.

35

Jealousy

"Now when Rachel saw that she bore Jacob no children, she became jealous of her sister; and she said to Jacob, 'Give me children, or else I die.' Then Jacob's anger burned against Rachel, and he said, 'Am I in the place of God, who has withheld from you the fruit of the womb?'" (Genesis 30:1-2).

Jealousy is an intense desire colored by distrust and suspicion because somebody has something you want. We can be jealous about any of the following, to give just a few examples:

● the way she looks. "Did you see those tight jeans?"

● his ability in sports. "Well, running is all he ever does. I could win the mile race, too, if I didn't have to work at the store every day."

● her boyfriend. "It's just his way of being nice, I guess. Nobody else would ask her out."

● his car. "Now don't get me wrong, Chevys are OK. But if I had that much money to throw around, I'd get something a little classier. Why, that looks like something his grandmother would pick out."

● her new outfit. "I saw that dress at Maxi's, too. It is a cute style, but I don't think the color is right for her."

● his money. "Would you look at that showoff? Pays for

137

his lunch with a twenty-dollar bill. It's a cinch he doesn't have to work for it like I do. Probably his dad just hands the stuff to him."

● her victory. "How did she manage to get the lead part in the school play? I have heard rumors that she's a pet in Mr. Smithers's class. And she's always off running errands for him."

● his freedom. "Boy, I couldn't get away with that—messing around at the lake all night. I'd hate to see his grades. He surely can't keep up."

Jealousy prevents us from enjoying the happiness and good fortune of others. The joy of victories should be shared with the people around us. Instead, many times one person's gift is another's irritation. Jealousy can so possess our thinking that we can't even see straight. Events tumble out of focus. Minor details get blown out of proportion. Jealousy stifles us because it demands our full attention on something we can probably do nothing about anyway.

Our jealousy is also a slap at God. We're telling Him that He's doing a better job of taking care of someone else. We're rebuking Him for His provisions for us.

We need to recognize the symptoms of envy and deal with them right away. Let it grow over a period of time and you're almost stuck with it. Call it what it is. Confess to the Lord that you're just plain jealous. Then thank Him and praise Him for allowing this friend, acquaintance, or relative to receive that bit of success.

When you're dealing with another Christian, your cause for a sincere "Congratulations!" is even more urgent. Whatever benefits one of the Lord's children or His kingdom, benefits us all. In one way or another, we're all in this family together to see that our Lord receives the best of all we've got to offer Him.

Also check out: Anger, Bitterness, Bragging, Clothes, Competition, Criticism, Failure, Friends, Frustration, Greed, Happiness, Humility, Inferiority, Materialism, Pettiness, Selfishness, Success, Ungratefulness.

36

Judgment

"Now if any man builds upon the foundation with gold, silver, precious stones, wood, hay, straw, each man's work will become evident; for the day will show it, because it is to be revealed with fire; and the fire itself will test the quality of each man's work. If any man's work which he has built upon it remains, he shall receive a reward. If any man's work is burned up, he shall suffer loss; but he himself shall be saved, yet so as through fire" (1 Corinthians 3:12-15).

John Aguilar admitted to Geoff that he was scared. That's the reason he kept making excuses about attending church with him. The preacher might mention Judgment Day or hell. Subjects like that made John uncomfortable. He was pretty sure happenings like that weren't real. But just the same. . . .

As he talked it over with Geoff, he realized it was like that summer that the logging mill where Mr. Aguilar worked closed down. There had been rumors flying for months: "The mill's going to close down." At first there was almost a panic among the two thousand workers and their families. But when nothing happened and the mill kept producing lumber as fast as ever, almost everyone forgot the scare.

141

But John's dad told the family they'd better get ready. He had seen a whole town wiped out before when a company chose to close the one industry's doors. They began to save their money, Mr. Aguilar scouted out nearby counties and states for alternate jobs, and Mrs. Aguilar signed up for a typing and bookkeeping class, just in case. And sure enough, one day the manager marched in and announced that this was the last week. What seemed so impossible was happening, and the workers were bitter. Why didn't they have more warning? What had they done to be treated like this? What would they do now?

John wondered if he was being smart by ignoring the rumors that a day to be judged was coming. He had no idea how he stood before such an awesome being as God. Should he investigate? Did he need to prepare? He sure hated to be like one of those workers who were caught by surprise when it was too late.

John is right to do some serious thinking about the matter. A person ought to know where his choices in life will lead. A warning of what's up ahead is only fair. Here's a quick survey of what we all should know about judgment.

Jesus is the judge. "For not even the Father judges any one, but He has given all judgment to the Son" (John 5:22). No wonder it's of crucial importance that we know Him as our Savior and Lord.

God's judgment has already come. "He who believes in Him is not judged; he who does not believe has been judged already, because he has not believed in the name of the only begotten Son of God" (John 3:18). Although unbelievers haven't yet tasted the consequences of that judgment, their verdict right now is "Guilty!" That's why good works can't save us. Without a personal acquaintance with the judge, we're doomed.

Judgment Day will be terrifying for unbelievers. "And if anyone's name was not found written in the book of life, he was thrown into the lake of fire" (Revelation 20:15). We human beings don't like words like that. We'd rather ignore them, ridicule them, or discredit them. But what if each word is literally true? I'd sure want to know, now, not only for my sake, but also for the sake of lots of others whom I care about.

If you were speeding down a steep mountain highway and suddenly you noticed a sign that warned of a dangerous curve ahead, you'd sure slow down and keep a watch out for that curve. You certainly wouldn't consider that a negative roadsign, either. It's a positive guide to keep you from destroying yourself.

Christians do not face this final judgment. "Truly, truly, I say to you, he who hears My word, and believes Him who sent Me, has eternal life, and does not come into judgment, but has passed out of death into life" (John 5:24). That information should cheer up John Aguilar. We all should thank and praise our God for this good news.

But each Christian's works will be examined. Read again the passage from 1 Corinthians 3 at the beginning of this devotional. Every follower of Christ will spend eternity in heaven. But some of us won't have much in the way of rewards or "crowns" to present to Him. That's because we used our earthly resources for worthless (to Him) pursuits. Our "good deeds" need to originate in God's mind, not out of our mixed motives (*see* Ephesians 2:10).

Also check out: Atheism, Boldness, Death, Disobedience, Doubt, Fear, Future, Purpose, Uncertainty, Worry, Zeal.

37

Love

"Love is patient, love is kind, and is not jealous; love does not brag and is not arrogant, does not act unbecomingly; it does not seek its own, is not provoked, does not take into account a wrong suffered, does not rejoice in unrighteousness, but rejoices with the truth; bears all things, believes all things, hopes all things, endures all things. Love never fails" (1 Corinthians 13:4-8a).

Can we make ourselves love someone? Or are we just hopeless robots chained to emotions that toss us to and fro?

Jesus gave a *command* that we love others, especially fellow believers. How can we do that? Some people rub us the wrong way. Some don't share any of our interests. Others have hurt us or someone close to us. Then there are those we just don't know well enough to "love." How do we love such people?

We love by doing loving deeds. Do you have a strained relationship with someone? Try to find out what *he or she* would consider to be a loving act. It might be getting your hair cut or washing the dishes. How about keeping your part of the house straightened or helping at the car wash? Actions like those can stir up God's deep well of love-springs that He's poured into our hearts (Romans 5:5).

Suppose you and your family moved to the Mojave

Desert. You find there a nice home with everything you need for a comfortable existence, except for water. Your family is desperate. They can't live without having water piped into the house.

Then you discover that someone built an enormous well right in your back yard with enough water available to last a lifetime and more. But it's all sealed up. There are no faucets, no pipes, no lines. How would you get that water to the house? Suppose you call the company who put in the well and they say, "Sorry, that's your problem. We just put in wells. You've got to get them flowing."

Somehow you'd find a way. You could build a line, put a fire hydrant at every corner, or whatever it took.

Everyone who believes in Christ as Savior has the Holy Spirit within him with His inexhaustible supply of love. We need to build enough channels, enough pipes, enough plumbing, to release that love flow to the folks around us.

We love by sharing our honors and privileges. Instead of saying, "Hey, Mom, Dad, guess what? I'm such a smart kid that I made the honor roll again," you say, "Thank you so much for providing the home environment and encouragement I needed to excel in my classes."

We love by sharing our name and reputation. Could you help that one you need to show love to by putting in a recommendation for a job or other type of position? Would you invite him to join your circle of friends for a special outing?

We love both by providing for needs and by allowing another to supply our own needs. Baking a cake as well as receiving a cake can be an opportunity for love to be demonstrated.

We love by listening. There are stories to tell, experiences to explain. All this is part of building bridges of love. We need to know not only that people hurt, but also *why* they hurt.

We love by touching. Jesus reached out His hands to many. He could heal with just a word, but He showed compassion with a physical touch on the hand, shoulder, or eyes—even on leprous skin. Holy hugs and holy kisses are Christian expressions of love.

We also love by leaving alone. There are times to give a friend some breathing and growing space. Love isn't possessive or touchy. But always leave with the door open. Let him know you'll be right back when he needs you.

We love by being accountable. Are you committed to a church, to a Bible study group, or to a youth group? We all need believers to meet with so that we can worship together and talk over our troubles and joys. Do you measure your commitment to other believers by what you get out of them or by what you can give?

We love by communicating one-to-one. A man told me recently, "You need to deal with individuals eyeball to eyeball, big toe to big toe, face to face."

We love by telling others about our faith. We show that we care by telling others all we know about how to know God through Jesus Christ. Be willing and able to explain why you go to church and how you became a Christian, and be honest about your struggles and joys along the Christian walk.

Also check out: Apathy, Bitterness, Family, Friends, Marriage, Restitution.

38

Lying

"Therefore, laying aside falsehood, speak truth, each one of you, with his neighbor, for we are members of one another. . . . Let no unwholesome word proceed from your mouth, but only such a word as is good for edification according to the need of the moment, that it may give grace to those who hear" (Ephesians 4:25, 29).

Eric is an addict. You know the type. He told his mother that he was late for school because his brother took too long in the shower. The truth is he overslept.

He told Mrs. Reynolds he was late to class because he stopped to help a child who'd fallen off her bike. Actually, he'd been in the men's room, trying to comb his hair just right.

Eric explained to the coach that he struck out because the sun rays bounced off the mechanics shop window. The truth is that he misjudged the curveball.

He told his dad that his homework was done; it wasn't, but he wanted to watch T.V. He told Crystal that he had to drop the basketball team to find a job, but he never made the cut.

Eric lives in a dream world. He's a chronic liar.

Lying is a lot like bragging. Those who accept themselves as they are find no need to lie. That's the first clue to understanding why a person lies.

Eric doesn't enjoy being just a second-string baseball player. So the coach told him how to improve. He needs to run, lift weights, and spend hours at hitting practice. Eric either has to accept the fact that he's second string or get busy working out. Instead, he opts for a third choice. He lies. He complains about his lousy breaks, how the coach doesn't like him, and how his teammates treat him to get him rattled. Eric's been saying those things so long that I think he really believes them.

The tragedy is that Eric has so few friends. The reason is obvious. No one knows who he is. He's so phony that those who do get close to him do so for the wrong reasons. Suppose Crystal believed his excuses and felt sorry for him. As their friendship grew, sooner or later she'd discover the obvious truth. The Eric she thought she liked doesn't even exist.

Speaking the truth does have limitations. It won't guarantee that everyone will like you. A visitor from a foreign country remarked that we Americans have an unusual trait. We can't stand to have anyone dislike us. Most of us are crushed if it happens. But he said that in his culture, it doesn't bother the people at all. That's why they aren't tempted with all the crazy fads and products that we are that are supposed to make us "popular," "loved," and "accepted by all."

Being truthful doesn't guarantee success, fame, or wealth, either. But truthfulness will result in fewer things to apologize for, fewer regrets, friends who accept you as you really are, less worry about your self-image, and, most of all, an honest life-style you don't have to be ashamed of, no matter who examines it—even if it's God.

Also check out: Bragging, Depression, Doubt, Failure, Friends, Frustration, Humility, Inconsistency, Inferiority, Jealousy, Self-worth, Self-control, Success.

39

Marriage

"And He answered and said, 'Have you not read, that He who created them from the beginning made them male and female, and said, "For this cause a man shall leave his father and mother, and shall cleave to his wife; and the two shall become one flesh"? Consequently they are no more two, but one flesh. What therefore God has joined together, let no man separate'" (Matthew 19:4-6).

Suzanne Conley thought it would be an easy assignment. Her senior Contemporary Living class was supposed to prepare a term paper on marriage. Suzanne figured that could be done with one or two nights at the library. But then came the catch. Each student had to interview at least five married couples.

Suzanne was nervous. How do you convince people to let you ask them questions about their marriages? But it didn't turn out to be as tough as she feared. Her parents agreed and suggested she ask their good friends who taught their Sunday school class. Then her grandmother told her about a couple she knew who'd been married for over fifty years. The youth pastor lined her up with a newlywed couple and one who had two small children. Armed with a notebook and tape recorder, she ventured out on her assignments.

Then came the hard part. She had to condense all those

interviews into some orderly fashion. She was elated to find five main points.

First, just because everything doesn't turn out as you expected does not mean you married the wrong person.

Mrs. Conley imagined settling down in a country home to raise at least five kids and grow a huge garden. But marriage to Mr. Conley turned out to be helping to feed farm animals, riding behind a grain drill, and driving a hay truck. She even helped put new shingles on the barn and mend fences. It was not the romantic picture she had envisioned.

One day she poured out her self-pity to a friend. Her friend told her, "You've got the right man and the wrong ideas. Don't let your wrong ideas dictate your marriage."

Second, most conflicts center on what she thinks versus what he does.

Mrs. Schilling admitted that she and Mr. Schilling argued most about how silly he acted out in public sometimes. He loved to crack jokes and tease waitresses. When she mentioned it to him, he always replied, "Stop worrying so much. You need to relax and enjoy life more." After fifty-three years, Mrs. Schilling has learned to allow her husband the freedom to be himself, and he's even funnier than ever.

Third, money is a major problem.

"It's a good thing you didn't come interview us at the end of the month," Linda Ramsey said. "We always go round and round about which bills to pay and what happened to the money. And the two little ones add to the budgeting problem. Even when Rob gets a bonus or raise, we find ourselves disagreeing about what to do with it."

Fourth, sex doesn't always come naturally.

The newlyweds told Suzanne of some of their premarital counseling. "The pastor was right. You've got to talk it over when something bothers you. This is an area where each partner needs to show consideration and sensitivity. We can sure see now why God advised that this act best grows and matures within the bounds of a lifetime vow of faithfulness."

Fifth, a marriage partner can be the fastest spur to spiritual growth.

"God uses Penny to soften me up and make me more attentive to people's needs," Gary said. "If it weren't for her, I'd barge right through life never knowing how many folks I had offended."

"And the Lord uses Gary to help me be more decisive," Penny said. "I can never make up my mind. Gary forces me to think things through and then decide. Sometimes I resent what I call his pushiness, but overall I realize what a better person I am because of his influence."

The report was one-sided in a way, because only those who were willing to work at building their marriages took the time to talk to Suzanne. But that was a lesson in itself for Suzanne. She saw what loving and influential people those couples were by their choosing to change when need be, build and rebuild, and keep going toward the goal of a stable family and close companionship.

Also check out: Compromise, Dating, Family, Forgiveness, Future, Love, Sexuality, Vocation.

40

Materialism

"Do not lay up for yourselves treasures upon earth, where moth and rust destroy, and where thieves break in and steal. But lay up for yourselves treasures in heaven, where neither moth nor rust destroys, and where thieves do not break in or steal; for where your treasure is, there will your heart be also" *(Matthew 6:19-21)*.

On Keith's top bunk lies a single lens reflex camera and telephoto lens (value $600). Against the far wall of his room stands a nineteen-inch color television ($400), and hooked up to it is a video game computer set (about $460). Then he has a pool table ($400), a stereo and earphones ($600), and a weight bench with weights ($150).

Keith's closet is full, too. He has a couple pair of tennis shoes ($40 each), football shoes ($45), hiking boots ($70), and thongs ($7.50 each because only Lightning Bolt would do). A colorful array of $25 knit shirts hangs neatly between $30 designer jeans. Surely Keith is one happy kid.

Not really—in fact, he's been pouting for days. There's a motorcycle he wants, and his dad says no.

Materialism becomes our life focus when things are more important than people, when we're always wanting something new or better. This disease can so possess a person that the occupation with acquiring some material thing becomes a detriment to social and spiritual growth.

How can you tell if this is a problem in your life? Here are some of the symptoms:

Severe Gimmeitus. If your friend (or enemy) has a certain thing, you suddenly discover you must have it, too. Look around your bedroom. Why do you have the items there? How many of them did you decide totally on your own that you wanted and needed?

Financial Daydreamums. Whenever your mind is free to think about whatever it chooses, what subjects pop up most often? That's where your actions will be sooner or later.

Robotus Depressionarus. In the chronic forms, this ailment shows a sufferer mutely pacing from one fad to another. The victim rarely smiles and has lost all eye twinkle.

But cheer up, thing-lovers everywhere, there are cures.

Cure #1: Spend a month in the woods. That's right. Grab a sleeping bag, a friend, a tent, and some food, and explore the great outdoors. Breathe in some fresh mountain air; cope with wilderness trails and survival without electricity. You'll make startling discoveries such as the fact that you can wear the same clothes two days in a row. One pair of shoes is sufficient. You go for days without worrying who made the Top Ten. And wonder of wonders, you may go clean cold turkey off media highs. There are many creative variations on this cure, but you get the idea.

Cure #2: Make a list of all your major possessions. These would be the sort of things you'd grab first if your house caught on fire. Now, one at a time, stick them in a storage room, closet, or other out-of-the-way place. Leave them there a month. Then, take inventory. Did you survive (great) (OK) (barely made it) (sneaked it out a week early)?

Cure #3: With that same list of major possessions, ask these questions: How easily could I share this with friends and not constantly worry that it would get ruined? Does anyone else but me get any benefit from this? If I had to get rid of this or leave it behind in order to fulfill some higher purpose, would I be willing?

Also check out: Clothes, Frustration, Greed, Griping, Happiness, Jealousy, Peer Pressure, Purpose, Selfishness, Ungratefulness.

41

Motives

"Let us therefore be diligent to enter that rest, lest anyone fall through following the same example of disobedience. For the word of God is living and active and sharper than any two-edged sword, and piercing as far as the division of soul and spirit, of both joints and marrow, and able to judge the thoughts and intentions of the heart. And there is no creature hidden from His sight, but all things are open and laid bare to the eyes of Him with whom we have to do" (Hebrews 4:11-13).

The football injury kept Ben on his back for a week. Every evening, several of his teammates stopped by to bring homework or chat about the day's events.

"Isn't that nice how those fellows are so willing to help you out, Ben," his mother remarked, "especially since we're still pretty new here?"

Ben nodded. It was pleasant to have the company. But he knew those boys a little bit better than his mom. They were more interested in being around Stacy, his sister, who he'd overheard them say was the cutest girl in the freshman class. Why else would they go out of their way for a second-string tackle?

Motives are those necessary desires and reasonings that

propel us to action. They're the subliminal switch that keeps us going. Such an important part of our personality and very being needs to be examined from time to time. Understanding your underlying motives for what you do will help you be a person of honesty and integrity.

Here's a simple motives test:

1. You struggled to get that *A* in biology because
   a. you were tired of hearing your parents gripe.
   b. you wanted to impress that boy/girl who sits behind you.
   c. your grandparents offered you a $25 bonus.
   d. you wanted to learn as much about biology as you could.
   e. all of the above.
2. You wash your hair every day because
   a. it's always dirty.
   b. you feel out of it all day if you don't have it looking as good as _____'s hair.
   c. you're trying to catch _____'s attention and you always want to look your best.
   d. your mother makes you do it.
3. You go to church every Sunday because
   a. the fellowship and teaching strengthen your spiritual growth.
   b. there's always the chance you'll get to talk with _____.
   c. your parents expect you to.
   d. you like singing in the choir.

Most of us try to hide our true motives, because they don't look as good as the public act we like people to see.

But God isn't fooled. He sees into the deepest part of us and still loves and accepts us. We should never be reluctant to inspect our motives openly before Him. That's how we get a clearer view of who we are.

Also check out: Anger, Bitterness, Bragging, Competition, Compromise, Criticism, Doubt, Friends, Grades, Humility, Jealousy, Love, Lying, Pride, Purpose.

42

Pettiness

"And the Pharisees and some of the scribes gathered together around Him when they had come from Jerusalem, and had seen that some of His disciples were eating their bread with impure hands, that is, unwashed. . . . And the Pharisees and the scribes asked Him, 'Why do Your disciples not walk according to the tradition of the elders, but eat their bread with impure hands?'" (Mark 7:1-2, 5).

"I am calling a family counsel meeting!" Carol announced.

"Not tonight!" Kerry said as he groaned. "I've got tennis practice."

Carol glared at her brother. "Mom, Dad, this is very important and the Cramer family rules say—"

"Yes, we know," Mr. Cramer said, "Anyone can call a meeting once before the regular monthly meeting, and all must attend. How about it, Kerry? And Christy? And Mom?"

Everyone agreed while Kerry muttered something about "It better be a quick one" as they gathered up their school books.

Right after dinner, Mr. Cramer brought the meeting to order. The first item of business was to go over the minutes of the previous meeting. Ten-year-old Christy stood to read.

"I move we suspend the reading of the minutes and proceed to the business at hand," Kerry said. "I'm late."

"I object," Carol replied. And according to the Cramer Rules of Order, the minutes were read.

Mr. Cramer continued. "Carol, now what is the urgent matter you need to bring before us? You have the floor."

"This is something that has been bugging me for years," she said, "and I think it's time that something was done about it. Exhibit A, the toothpaste tube. I refuse to share this smashed tube with Kerry anymore. He insists on squeezing at the top instead of the bottom. And he always leaves the lid off and a bunch of goo oozing out. It makes me sick."

"What?" Kerry's face was beet red. "For this I'm late for tennis? I can't believe it. I move we adjourn this meeting."

"Out of order," answered Mr. Cramer. "But Carol, this does seem a rather minor infraction for calling a special family council."

"Minor! Do you call this minor? How would you like to stare at this every morning?" She held up the smeared and smashed tube. "I think Kerry does it on purpose because he knows how much it irritates me."

"Now that's a more serious charge," Mr. Cramer said.

"Could you slow down, please?" Christy, the secretary, said. "I can't write that fast."

They waited a moment for Christy to catch up, and then Mr. Cramer asked, "Kerry, did you leave the tube like that?"

"But Dad, I don't think I even brushed my teeth this

morning. Carol took about a thirty-minute shower and I—"

"He lies, too!" Carol said with a glance back at her dad. "I think—"

"May the secretary say something?" Everyone turned to a sheepish-looking Christy. "I think I can explain. This morning I dropped the toothpaste and didn't pick it up right away. Then my towel fell over it, and when I got out of the shower I stepped on it. I cleaned up the mess on the floor, but I forgot to clean the tube. I'm sorry, Carol. I didn't know that's what you were upset about."

"Carol," said Mr. Cramer, "you owe your brother an apology."

"But what about all those other times?"

"Carol!"

"OK. I'm sorry, I guess."

At that meeting the Cramer rules were changed by executive decision to include an amendment stating that the agenda for specially called meetings had to be discussed with the chairman beforehand.

Pettiness, the excessive attention given to little irritations, can waste more time and energy than television commercials.

Also check out: Anger, Clothes, Criticism, Family, Friends, Frustration, Griping, Inconsistency, Motives, Ungratefulness.

43

Peer Pressure

"Nevertheless many even of the rulers believed in Him, but because of the Pharisees they were not confessing Him, lest they should be put out of the synagogue; for they loved the approval of men rather than the approval of God" (John 12:42-43).

Keren bought the blue dress with the lace and full skirt one summer when her family vacationed in Montana. The frilly dress looked so pretty on the rack, and her sister and mother said it looked even better on her. She wore it several times for special family gatherings as they traveled through the western states.

When they returned home to southern California, Keren hung the dress toward the back in her closet, with her winter coat. Why? All of a sudden it looked out of place. What would her friends think? ~~All they ever wore were jeans.~~ No one at Hoover High ever wore dresses. Even if they did, they wouldn't be the lace-and-full-skirt variety.

Peer pressure is that ever-present influence on your decisions exerted either intentionally or unintentionally by those your own age—your friends, those you go to school with, and so on. It's one of the strong forces in society; it can be like the power of a river's current. Most of us are easily swept along in its path without even realizing we're just moving along with the crowd. But even a swift river has that rock or two that won't budge. How can you be such a rock against the constant flow of peer pressure? For that matter, why should you even want to?

Conformity isn't necessarily wrong. All of Keren's friends have a fetish about keeping their teeth bright and white. They even bring their toothbrushes to school and brush after lunch in the restrooms. That standard certainly has a healthy result for Keren's crowd.

But in deciding when the crowd is wrong, you need some basis for absolute, unchanging truth. If you don't have it, you'll always feel you're living one step behind everybody as you try to keep step with the tug of your group.

There's only one absolute set of truth that can endure throughout your lifetime, the principles of God's Word, the Bible. When you know that wisdom, you'll always have a guide for your behavior.

A good rule is to have the boldness to question. Why does everyone want to do this? Is there a better way? Does another action make more sense? Will this bring more trouble than enjoyment? Will this bring harm or discomfort to someone outside our group?

Within the boundaries of God's Word, we really have a wide variety of choices to make as we live the abundant life Christ promised. Why narrow your life down to anything less? Someone needs to be a pacesetter. Why not you?

Valerie spent the first three years of high school doing everything she could to find approval with a certain group of girls. Even when they included her in their group for lunchtimes and slumber parties, however, she still felt very unsure that they really accepted her.

Then Valerie's older sister, Margene, invited her to a Bible study. Valerie went because she was so shocked to have Margene include her in anything. On the way to the study, Margene told Valerie how she had believed in Christ and was now trying to learn how to be His disciple.

At the Bible study, Valerie heard for the first time how God knew us inside out and was ready to receive us as His children without any efforts at change on our part. She learned that there was no use in trying to put something over on God. He knew the truth and still offered love. Valerie was visibly shaken by this unexpected news. She talked to the leader afterward and prayed that Christ would become her friend and Savior.

After that, Valerie no longer felt the pressure to prove herself to her friends. She relaxed and accepted herself and them as they were. And when she did that, she made more friends than ever in all kinds of groups. Now Valerie talks about her insights with girls on campuses all over the country as part of a Christian campus ministry.

Also check out: Boldness, Bragging, Clothes, Compromise, Dating, Drunkenness, Friends, Inconsistency, Inferiority, Purpose, Self-Control, Shyness, Uncertainty.

44

Pride

"Do not love the world, nor the things in the world. If any one loves the world, the love of the Father is not in him. For all that is in the world, the lust of the flesh and the lust of the eyes and the boastful pride of life, is not from the Father, but is from the world" (1 John 2:15-16).

To say a person "has no pride" isn't always a compliment. The intended meaning is usually that the individual does not care enough about himself and others to present himself in a decent manner in public. Our pride does motivate us to be social and pleasant and to strive for all kinds of worthwhile accomplishments. So our pride isn't all bad, in that sense.

But pride out of control can blind us and so twist us that we can't see ourselves and our relationships as they really are.

Benny thought he was the greatest. Just ask him. He was the best 190-pound wrestler, the best log roller, and the best linebacker in the history of Prairie High. He loves to tell about how he recovered the fumble during the championship game that led his team to victory.

Benny did recover that fumble. But Benny never took the time to see the films of the game. Others who did saw something else, too. Ken Holly played an outstanding game in the backfield: 123 yards rushing and 73 yards on pass receptions, including three touchdowns.

173

And Benny? He was beaten by a Camas Hill guard all
night long: no tackles, no assists, and three times the guard
ran over Benny to sack the quarterback. The actual play of
the fumble showed that Ken, who played end on defense,
hit the ball carrier hard and the ball popped loose. At the
same time up on the line, Benny got pounded into the dirt
again. But just before he hit the dirt, out of nowhere the
football squirted under him. Nice recovery, Benny. He
allowed a bit of gridiron luck to go to his head.

Pride *can* lead to a healthy self-respect of one's position
and skills, however. Marie seems to have a firm grasp of her
musical abilities.

"Hey, Marie, what's your band ranking?"

"I'm playing number one clarinette."

"Oh, yeah? What does it take to get there?"

"An hour's practice a day. There are lots of good players
in our orchestra, and I have to work hard to stay there. But
it's worth it to me. The competition has made me a better
player."

Marie has a beautiful plaque hanging on her bedroom
wall: "Superior, State Honor Orchestra, First Chair." She's
proud of it because she knows it didn't come easily for her.

We can make honest statements about our achievements
and enjoy them without falling into a false pride trap. That
kind of pride should then encourage us to cheerfully recognize
and acknowledge the accomplishments of others, too.

*Also check out: Anger, Bragging, Clothes, Competition,
Friends, Humility, Lying, Self-worth, Selfishness, Success,
Ungratefulness.*

45

Purpose

"Now I rejoice in my sufferings for your sake, and in my flesh I do my share on behalf of His body (which is the church) in filling up that which is lacking in Christ's afflictions. . . . And we proclaim Him, admonishing every man and teaching every man with all wisdom, that we may present every man complete in Christ. And for this purpose also I labor, striving according to His power, which mightily works within me" (Colossians 1:24, 28-29).

Is there anything you labor and strive for? In other words, what would you consider worth some pain and disciplined effort to achieve?

Sam, at 17, still isn't sure what he wants to do with his life. But he does know that he doesn't want to waste the years ahead. "I want to do something meaningful," he says. "I want my life to count."

He has been investigating various fields of study and what they offer, and he's dividing them into his own categories:

Fame

professional sports/radio, TV, announcing, acting, etc./politics

Money

medicine/law/stocks and bonds/real estate

Pleasure
forestry/sporting goods business/architecture
Service
teaching/counseling/mission work/ministry

But as Sam spent months thinking through each of these options and talking with people who were already there, he noticed that those he had labeled *Service* couldn't guarantee a life of purpose or accomplishment, and those he labeled as nonserving careers were used by many as ministry and serving professions. He was surprised and relieved that the nature or title of the work wasn't as important as certain attitudes and motivations inside.

With the help and encouragement of his youth pastor, Sam wrote down a set of general guidelines that he felt defined his purpose as a Christian.

1. Because I belong to God, I will to do nothing that will dishonor His name.
2. Because I am a child of the King, I have a sure inheritance.
3. God is worthy of my best efforts. Any task will be done for His approval first of all.
4. I will venture through any open doors He wills and leave the results to Him.
5. As I plan my future and decide my goals, He and I understand that they are subject to His changes without prior notice.

Sam still has some choices to make, and they aren't easy. He was offered a basketball scholarship to the state university. His uncle suggested he come help him in his law office this summer. The youth pastor wants him to apply for an internship program at a friend's church in the university town. And he still can't decide on a major.

But Sam is going to take one step at a time. He's confident that some of the choices will be eliminated and others will increase in interest. It's just a matter of time and purpose.

Also check out: Apathy, Boldness, Boredom, Compromise, Depression, Failure, Family, Future, Grades, Motives, Success, Uncertainty, Victory, Vocation.

46

Restitution

"If therefore you are presenting your offering at the altar, and there remember that your brother has something against you, leave your offering there before the altar, and go your way; first be reconciled to your brother, and then come and present your offering. Make friends quickly with your opponent at law while you are with him on the way, in order that your opponent may not deliver you to the judge, and the judge to the officer, and you be thrown into prison. Truly I say to you, you shall not come out of there, until you have paid up the last cent" (Matthew 5:23-26).

The biology book slid down the stairs with the greatest of ease—bounce, hit, bounce, hit. By the time it reached the first-floor landing, the cover was ripped off, some pages were torn, and one page was missing. Bradley scowled. Biology wasn't his favorite subject, but this had been an accident. And Mr. Cummins was strict. He had warned them to return their books at the end of the semester in good condition "or else!"

Bradley knew "or else" meant a fine. He wasn't about to pay for replacing a biology book. So he carefully concealed his tattered mess from Mr. Cummins. He could always look on with Kim Frazier in class when he needed to, and he checked out a copy from the library for open book tests.

After finals, the students piled their books on Mr. Cummins's desk. Grades were mailed out the following week. But Bradley didn't receive his. There was some mix-up at school, a letter from the principal stated. When Bradley reported to the office, they told him he couldn't get his report card until he talked with Mr. Cummins. *Oh, brother, the book has come to haunt me,* he thought. He was right. Eight dollars later, he got his grades.

Making restitution for our failures is tough. It calls for courage, a good dose of humility, and honesty.

The checker at the Pizza Palace gives you five dollars too much in change. You sure could use that extra five. Besides, they'd never know.

You borrow a sleeping bag for winter camp and keep forgetting to return it. Your friend hasn't mentioned it in quite a while, so you hate to go to the bother of bringing it up yourself.

You back out of a dark parking lot and put a dent in a Cadillac door. In panic you floorboard it out of there without a second glance. *Did anyone see me? Should I report it?* The worries grow.

It's not worth it. Restitution keeps your conscience clear, your character strong, and your witness for Jesus Christ pure. But do it quickly. The sooner, the better. Do it thoroughly. Reimburse every bit. Admit your mistake and determine not to get yourself in that fix again.

Also check out: Depression, Disobedience, Drunkenness, Failure, Family, Forgiveness, Friends, Guilt, Humility, Inconsistency, Lying.

47

Self-worth ✞

"Therefore do not be ashamed of the testimony of our Lord, or of me His prisoner; but join with me in suffering for the gospel according to the power of God, who has saved us, and called us with a holy calling, not according to our works, but according to His own purpose and grace which was granted us in Christ Jesus from all eternity. . . . For this reason I also suffer these things, but I am not ashamed; for I know whom I have believed and I am convinced that He is able to guard what I have entrusted to Him until that day" (2 Timothy 1:8-9, 12).

Paul was in jail when he wrote those words. You remember Paul, don't you? He spent over thirty years spreading the story of Jesus Christ throughout the known world. What did that get him? Persecution, ridicule, and rejection.

But there were rewards, too. Thousands received Christ; hundreds of churches sprang up.

But now he sat in a prison in Rome. Scholars say Second Timothy is the last letter Paul wrote. He knew the end was near.

What would you write in your last letter? Could you be as confident as Paul that you had "fought the good fight, . . . finished the course, . . . kept the faith"?

Paul wasn't ashamed to admit he believed in Jesus, even though that is what got him into trouble. That's why certain leaders hated him. The scholars in Athens put him down. Those same beliefs got him arrested.

Paul knew that God's power had completely changed his life. If God hadn't helped him to understand the truth, he still would have been out in left field, fighting on the wrong side. Now he could even face death because he was confident of who he was and who he belonged to. He wasn't even ashamed to be found in the demeaning pit of a jail.

More important to Paul than anything—who his friends were, where he went to school, what his family connections were—was the fact that he knew God. He didn't just know a few facts about God; he hadn't merely memorized some Bible verses; he didn't just pass on comments he had heard from others. Paul knew God on a personal basis.

Paul had his life together; he had self-worth. You can't buy that in an aerosol can. No one can give it to you. Self-worth is looking at yourself with a serious, calm honesty, both the good and the bad, and saying, "Lord, thank You for making me. I appreciate the privilege of living out this particular life."

Self-worth is available to anyone. How do I know? Because I know Someone who thinks you are so important that He died for you. This same One thinks you're worth preparing a permanent home for. He hurts to think of life in eternity without you. Isn't it about time you showed your gratitude for such a person?

Self-worth is knowing who you are before God and finding peace and contentment in that position. With that kind of relationship, you could sit in prison with Paul and even sing.

Also check out: Bragging, Clothes, Competition, Criticism, Depression, Failure, Grades, Guilt, Inferiority, Jealousy, Lying, Shyness, Success, Ungratefulness.

48

Self-control

"But the fruit of the Spirit is love, joy, peace, patience, kindness, goodness, faithfulness, gentleness, self-control; against such things there is no law. Now those who belong to Christ Jesus have crucified the flesh with its passions and desires. If we live by the Spirit, let us also walk by the Spirit. Let us not become boastful, challenging one another, envying one another" (Galatians 5:22-26).

"Oh, I'm sorry. It's just, well, I couldn't help myself."

Have you heard a statement like that? Have you made it yourself?

Self-control is that ability to guide one's thoughts and actions in the direction of a previously determined goal. We don't have to look too far to see lives that seem out of control.

Tari eats too much. B. J. always cusses. Jay is in another fight. Joanna is daydreaming about boys again. Vance can't survive without a pinch of chewing tobacco. "I just can't help it," they all claim.

What they really mean is that they don't have the will, the strong-enough desire, to break the habits they've allowed to control them. A better statement would be, "I cannot will to stop." If only there were some way to reach in and flip our "on" and "off" will switch.

All who believe in and confess Jesus as God's Son receive the power of the Holy Spirit within them. From that point on, our purpose should be to allow Him freedom to work His power and control within us. That is what it means to be filled with the Spirit. One way we can know if that is happening is to watch results. Are you growing in love? Are you finding peace? Do you have self-control?

Without His help, our case is hopeless. Like Paul, we will find ourselves "doing the very thing I do not wish" (Romans 7:20).

Life out of control is frightening. But the good news is that you can help yourself if—if you're willing to admit your need to God and seek His way.

Also check out: Boldness, Inconsistency, Lying, Peer Pressure, Purpose, Self-worth, Sexuality.

49

Selfishness

"When God saw their deeds, that they turned from their wicked way, then God relented concerning the calamity which He had declared He would bring upon them. And He did not do it. But it greatly displeased Jonah, and he became angry" (Jonah 3:10—4:1).

The Palmers were giving the biggest party of the year, a luau in honor of their son, Tony's, acceptance to the university. Dreena couldn't understand why her sister, Pam, had been invited but she hadn't.

She realized Pam was closer to Tony's age, but they'd all been friends. She tried to forget the hurt as she helped her mother sew up the lovely, flowered kimono Pam would wear. They helped her pick out new sandals and a red camellia for her hair.

Mom, Dad, and Dreena played Monopoly the night of the party. *Great fun,* thought Dreena as she yawned. *You'd think I was twelve instead of sixteen.*

A week later, Dreena saw Mrs. Palmer at the department store. Dreena had only met her once and wasn't sure if she'd know her. But she was surprised to hear "Dreena, Dreena Carlson, is that you?"

"Yes, aren't you Mrs. Palmer?"

"I sure am. Tony talks of you often. So sorry you've been ill. We missed you at the party."

"What?"

"Oh, Pam explained to us all about it, why you couldn't come and all."

"But, I didn't know I was invited."

Mrs. Palmer looked startled and then said, "I knew I should have sent two invitations. I sure hope I haven't caused any trouble. I know I wrote out both names."

Dreena stared after Mrs. Palmer in amazement. She couldn't believe such a thing from her own sister.

Later Dreena learned that Pam had felt threatened by Tony's growing attentions to the younger sister. She wanted Tony for herself.

Selfishness can afflict even pious people. Jonah was a prophet of God. God told him to go warn the Ninevites to repent or they would be destroyed. But Jonah had a better idea. Why didn't God destroy them right then? After all, they deserved it. They were violent and cruel people. He hesitated about telling them such a message because there was just a chance that they'd listen. Then what? He knew God well enough to know He would forgive them and let them live.

Of course, that is just what happened. And Jonah was furious. How could God extend His loving grace to such people as that? It just wasn't fair.

As Jonah pouted up on a hill overlooking the city, a plant suddenly grew up and provided shade from the hot sun. Jonah calmed down a bit and lay down for a nap. But a worm ate the plant and Jonah was angry again. He didn't care if he died.

Jonah was so selfish that he cared more about a plant than he did about a whole city full of people who needed mercy.

Also check out: Anger, Apathy, Boredom, Family, Fear, Friends, Greed, Griping, Humility, Inconsistency, Love, Materialism, Motives, Ungratefulness.

50

Sexuality

"How beautiful you are, my darling, How beautiful you are! Your eyes are like doves."

"How handsome you are, my beloved, and so pleasant! Indeed, our couch is luxuriant!" (Song of Solomon 1:15-16).

Sometimes we forget that it was all God's idea in the first place. He created males in all their maleness and females in all their femaleness. Together they form a perfect match, a complementary pair made in God's image.

Both have equal standing before God as His children, but both are very different. You don't need to be told that. You stumbled onto that pleasant discovery several years ago. Males and females were made to be companions for one another. Eve was created because Adam wasn't satisfied with making friends with trees and birds, no matter how perfectly made. Of course, there's always a Pioneer Sam (or Samantha) who will argue with Adam's weakness, but he didn't mind admitting it.

It was God's idea that a man and woman live together and work at building a loving, caring community called family. He knew what He was doing when He created physical bodies that would attract and provide the means for reproducing a whole new line of miniature males and females.

But with that crunch into the forbidden fruit came the need for boundaries. We've been arguing about that ever since, too. Our sexual drives need to be controlled and properly channeled or we mess up the whole, beautiful plan.

God insists that sexual relations remain the exclusive property of couples who have promised faithfulness to one another "until death do us part." That is still the ideal, and, believe it or not, many do reach it. Not only that, but they will also witness to the fact that one lover, one mate, proves to be the most satisfying arrangement.

But that does leave a problem or two. How do you deal with all those other attractive beings you keep bumping into in the course of a day? The Bible gives some suggestions. We are to treat young males as our brothers, older males as our fathers. Young females should be respected as sisters, older females as mothers. The implication is that the responsibility is on each of us to consider one another as more than just bodies of warm flesh. There are minds to explore, social interactions to enjoy, feelings to share, and interests and goals to work for together. And that's just the tip of the iceberg of the complexities of possible human interchanges.

The sophisticates of our day think they know more about sex than God. You'll be hearing a lot from them. But take time to listen to the other side, too. Our heavenly Father has a deep stake in our lives. He paid a heavy cost to free us from the kind of bondage we're so eager to get ourselves into. The least we can do is give Him a chance to prove His case.

Also check out: Compromise, Creation, Dating, Failure, Family, Forgiveness, Love, Marriage, Peer Pressure, Self-worth, Self-control, Trauma.

51

Shyness

"Thus Samuel brought all the tribes of Israel near, and the tribe of Benjamin was taken by lot. Then he brought the tribe of Benjamin near by its families, and the Matrite family was taken. And Saul the son of Kish was taken; but when they looked for him, he could not be found. Therefore they inquired further of the LORD, 'Has the man come here yet?' So the LORD said, 'Behold, he is hiding himself by the baggage'" (1 Samuel 10:20-22).

It was the first day of school, and Cory didn't even know which bus he was supposed to ride. He stood in line at the corner. He tried to look calm. But he could feel his cheeks turning that horrible, rosy pink color. *Just like a little kid,* Cory thought. *You'd think a high school kid could stand on a street corner without blushing.*

"Hey, freshman," a deep voice shouted, "What are you doing in our line? Seniors first."

A mortified Cory stepped back and considered a moment what his hopes were that he could hitch a ride on a freight train to Miami. But several kids soon shoved him up on the bus, and thirty long minutes later he entered his first day at Tampa High. Now to find room 238. He circled the administration building three times before he talked himself into asking someone for directions.

During P.E., he just about panicked when he couldn't get his locker open. One of the coaches finally came over and gave him a hand. Cory was sure all eyes were on him. During algebra, he missed receiving a book and couldn't follow the lesson. But he was too bashful to mention the oversight.

Some good things did happen, however. While sitting at one end of a cafeteria table, two cute girls sat nearby. He didn't get up until long after he was through eating, because he couldn't stand the thought of drawing their attention. He pretended to be writing notes on his class schedule.

Shyness hurts. A shy person is controlled by real or imagined fears that prevent any kind of social exertion under unfamiliar conditions. Kids like Cory are shy all the time, but others experience temporary bouts.

Sometimes a person becomes shy when he feels unworthy or reluctant for some reason to receive an honor. Remember King Saul in the First Samuel account. He hid behind the baggage when Samuel tried to appoint him Israel's first king.

Shyness can be the result of an unclear view of yourself as a likable personality. You're afraid to risk new relationships. But making a new friend, experiencing a new situation, or facing an unknown condition can produce strong character. It can also result in failure. So shyness can be a defense for the self-image, a protection against a potential threat to a tightly held position. But such safety can stifle mental, social, and spiritual growth.

In some instances, shyness can be a mask to hide a seething anger, bitterness, or violence. Such an individual may need professional counseling. At the least they need a caring friend who will allow them to unburden themselves of a lot of woes. They are possible time bombs who need to be diffused.

Cory decided his junior year that he was tired of being shy. He gave himself a pep talk each day in the bathroom mirror. "OK, Cory, you're going to win some and you're going to lose some today. It's no big deal." Each morning he had a goal of initiating a conversation with at least one person. It was a small step, but a brave one for Cory. By the end of the year, he even learned to laugh and joke with the girls about his horribly rosy pink cheeks.

Also check out: Boldness, Competition, Compromise, Depression, Failure, Fear, Frustration, Inferiority, Self-worth, Trauma, Zeal. You might also want to read the book Why Am I Shy?, *by Norman B. Rohrer and S. Philip Sutherland, Augsburg.*

52

Success

"Brethren, I do not regard myself as having laid hold of it yet; but one thing I do: forgetting what lies behind and reaching forward to what lies ahead, I press on toward the goal for the prize of the upward call of God in Christ Jesus. Let us therefore, as many as are perfect [mature], have this attitude; and if in anything you have a different attitude, God will reveal that also to you; however, let us keep living by that same standard to which we have attained" (Philippians 3:13-16).

Mandy worked hard to get a part in the church play. She spent long hours memorizing a whole scene and auditioned with ten other girls from the Community Church youth group. She could see this as an important opportunity to minister in front of hundreds of people. She believed in the message of the play and prayed that many would be inspired to a closer commitment to Christ by watching it. That's why she was so pleased when she learned she'd been chosen for the female lead.

Weeks and months of practice took her time and efforts. She gave her all. But some of the other participants weren't as dedicated. Even Darrell, the male lead, didn't know all his lines by the first dress rehearsal.

This is what worried Mandy more than anything else: Her most important scene came in response to Darrell's dramatic entrance. He never got it right in rehearsal.

Finally the big night arrived. Mandy was disappointed to find only 500 in the audience instead of the 1,000 they expected. Then Darrell arrived late and barely had time to apply makeup. Other than that, the scenes ran smoothly until—

Darrell's turn came for the build-up to the climax. But instead of lunging forward to argue with Mandy as he was supposed to, he backed up as if overwhelmed. That's when he stumbled on a chair and knocked down himself and another player. After that he was so flustered that he couldn't remember anything. The youth pastor finally walked on stage to help him, and they closed the play to the sympathetic laughs of the audience.

Mandy thought it was a disaster. Three months of hard work seemed wasted. But Mandy had forgotten something. She had been diligent to commit the project to God in all her planning, preparing, and action. But one more step is needed for any kind of spiritual success. She needed to commit the results to Him, too.

As we get older and begin to desire to give our best and use all our abilities to further the kingdom of God, we naturally must also deal with our desires for success. We want projects we do for Him to be as good as or better than anything we do for our school, our clubs, our community, or anyone else. That's good. He deserves our best effort. How do we deal with those desires?

First, bring your project or plan to God in thoughtful

prayer. Ask Him if He has any objections to the idea. Ask for His support. Examine all your motives for why you want to do it. Be honest.

Second, continue to commit all the details of planning and action to Him. Give close attention to all the necessary duties until the task is completed.

Third, commit the results to God. That's His department. He knows all about undependable people, unexpected, last-minute changes, and even the deliberate forces of evil that don't want you to succeed. He can see and work through it all to accomplish His perfect purpose.

Success isn't that elusive a goal when you try to understand human dealings from God's perspective.

Also check out: Boldness, Competition, Failure, Frustration, Future, Grades, Happiness, Motives, Pride, Purpose, Victory, Vocation, Zeal.

53

Suicide

"For not one of us lives for himself, and not one dies for himself; for if we live, we live for the Lord, or if we die, we die for the Lord; therefore whether we live or die, we are the Lord's. For to this end Christ died and lived again, that He might be Lord both of the dead and of the living. But you, why do you judge your brother? Or you again, why do you regard your brother with contempt? For we shall all stand before the judgment seat of God. . . . So then each one of us shall give account of himself to God" (Romans 14:7-10, 12).

Everybody knew who Jim was, of course. His brother, Tad, was captain of the Ranger football team. Jim's friend, Travis, was a sophomore, too, and had a reputation for recklessness. That's why the first stories around explained it as a tragic accident.

Neither Jim nor Travis had any academic drives. Their main delight was to cruise the main street with long hair flying, shirts off, and plenty of curbside teasing with the girls. On Friday and Saturday nights, they got drunk at beer parties down along Cottonwood Creek.

"One mile curve" was its name. At the left, a sheer, sixty-foot drop slid to the rocky bottom of the creek. Right at that corner was a scenic overlook. That is, it was scenic in the daytime. At night it was just a dark place to park.

Jim and Travis boasted several times that they were going to fly right over that curve and kill themselves. Their friends didn't take them seriously. After all, wasn't it just the beer talking? But on November 22, 1980, they bragged that this was the night. They made a suicide pact in front of several witnesses.

Startled teen onlookers gasped as they watched the green Ford pickup crash the guardrail and burst into flame on the way to the bottom. A loud explosion followed. Jim was killed instantly. Travis was thrown from the vehicle and survived, but he lost his left leg. It was tragic, all right, but it was no accident.

Travis is now serving a term at a Colorado correctional authority juvenile facility.

Suicide happens under many widely different circumstances and to all types of people. That it happens so often to young people is a reason to be alert to the signs. Do you have any friends who are so depressed or discouraged that they have mentioned to you the option of suicide? If so, please consider carefully the following suggestions.

Take it seriously. Don't assume they are just trying to get attention. That may be true, but don't take any chances. Suicidal people can be driven to the brink by ridicule or other insensitive responses to their pleas for help or announcements of their intentions. Let them talk out their feelings. Help them verbalize how they see their situations.

Remind them of the wider scope of life. They are probably trapped into "tunnel vision." They can only see a small portion of what's going on, either by choice or by the crush of overwhelming (to them) temporary circumstances. A

relationship may have been severed, a goal didn't material-
ize, a dream was busted, or they may suffer from the endless
boredom of a purposeless life.

Take time to help them think through the immediate
problems and then beyond. Even if you can't come up with
solutions, help them know you care and will stand by them.
Life has many stages, many seasons. There's always an
alternative to suicide. Would a change in environment
help? Would a simple talk with offended parties improve
the situation? Does the friend know what Christ has to
offer? Is there an experienced counselor available?

Warn them of possible consequences. This needs to be done
in a caring and loving way, but it must be done. What other
lives will be affected if this one is purposely taken? What
opportunities and surprise solutions will be needlessly left
unexplored? Do they have any idea what is ahead of them in
the next life? Are they prepared to face that unknown?

A Christian's life belongs to God. Our heavenly Father is
Lord of our lives—and our deaths. We need to be careful
when we willfully choose to destroy this gift of living for
Him. Knowing Christ should be filling our lives with
abundance (John 10:10), peace (Romans 5:1), and the
adventure of receiving a special assignment (Matthew
28:19-20). The time, place, and means of our deaths should
belong to Him.

*Also check out: Apathy, Boldness, Boredom, Death, Depres-
sion, Failure, Frustration, Guilt, Happiness, Illness, Judgment, Love, Purpose, Self-worth, Self-control, Selfishness,
Success, Trauma, Trials, Ungratefulness.*

54

Trauma

"Then when Herod saw that he had been tricked by the magi, he became very enraged, and sent and slew all the male children who were in Bethlehem and in all its environs, from two years old and under, according to the time which he had ascertained from the magi. Then that which was spoken through Jeremiah the prophet was fulfilled, saying, 'A voice was heard in Ramah, weeping and great mourning, Rachel weeping for her children; and she refused to be comforted, because they were no more'" (Matthew 2:16-18).

Carolyn bit her lip. She refused to cry. For over six years she hadn't allowed herself even a tear. And now was certainly not the time to give in. She stared at the walls in the nurse's office. The principal had just informed her that she would not be allowed to participate in the graduation exercises unless she wore a dress. She refused.

Carolyn hadn't always worn those scruffy-looking jeans and T-shirts everywhere she went. She used to enjoy wearing dresses and ruffled blouses. But that's when she was much younger. That was back before she was sent to the Walsh home to live.

By the time Carolyn was twelve years old, both her mother and father had died. Since there were no other relatives to claim her, the court ordered her to live with Mr. and Mrs. Walsh, a great uncle and great aunt on her father's side. They had a nice house, plenty of money, a daughter away at college, and no other children. It should have been a perfect solution for Carolyn, but it wasn't.

At first Carolyn was just annoyed. Mr. Walsh had a habit of hugging and kissing her too much. But one weekend Mrs. Walsh attended a conference in another city. One evening while Carolyn was washing the dishes, Mr. Walsh grabbed her from behind. Carolyn screamed. He held tight.

Carolyn protested with all her might. He wouldn't stop. "It's that pretty dress, honey," he said. "You look so pretty in it."

The dress was torn. Carolyn cried for days. Never again would she wear a dress. Never again would she cry.

Incidents of trauma in a young life can make deep scars that affect all of life's decisions and patterns of behavior. Unless Carolyn finds help and healing for that painful experience in her past, she'll remain an emotional cripple.

Not everyone reacts to trauma in the same way. Some have an amazing ability to grow right over and through it with a strength of character that is a wonderful blessing to everyone they meet. Others require years of intense counseling, medical attention, and other professional care to survive such an ordeal.

Six years is a long time to allow a wound like that to fester. But Carolyn finally did get the help she needed. Ruth Simpson, her Sunday school teacher and a secretary in the school's counseling department, tried to get Carolyn to talk about herself. Eventually she gained Carolyn's confidence, and Carolyn spilled out her story.

Ruth talked with the principal, and he allowed an exception in Carolyn's case, so she graduated in her usual attire. But she did have on brand new jeans and a modest, printed, button down blouse. Everyone remarked at the change in Carolyn.

Ruth Simpson's caring and Carolyn's growing as a young lady and whole personality didn't stop there. Five years later, Ruth watched Carolyn walk down the aisle as calm as can be in a gorgeous, lacy, white gown.

Why did Carolyn's episode have a happy ending?

She found someone to talk to. Ruth Simpson was a mature, trusted friend who could listen to all the ugly details and still accept her as a person capable of being loved. Ruth also knew the power of Christ and explained to Carolyn His offer of help. Ruth was readily available when the healing tears began to flow again and the bitter memories brought self-torment.

She found an avenue for examining what she really felt about herself. She learned to stop blaming herself and saw how she could be free from the fears and the confusion.

She devoured every Scripture verse that dealt with God's compassion and power. Her need led her to the One who came to set captives like Carolyn free.

She determined to get on with her life. She accepted the fact that she'd always live with some residue of after-effects. But she threw off her tough scowl, gradually experimented with her wardrobe, and realized that not all males were potential Mr. Walshes.

Also check out: Bitterness, Depression, Failure, Family, Guilt, Self-worth, Sexuality, Suicide, Trials, Victory.

55

Trials ✱ *(handwritten)*

"Therefore we do not lose heart, but though our outer man is decaying, yet our inner man is being renewed day by day. For momentary, light affliction is producing for us an eternal weight of glory far beyond all comparison" (2 Corinthians 4:16-17). → Another Fight with your brother or sister. *(handwritten)*

A mall to shop in; but no money. *(handwritten)*

Homework that just won't quit. *(handwritten)*

A pop quiz in ~~chemistry.~~ science. *(handwritten)*

~~Choir~~ *(handwritten)*

A flat tire on the way to ~~band~~ practice.

A Friend who just doesn't understand. *(handwritten)*

~~A fist fight to break up at the game.~~

A mother who won't let you go out on Friday night.

A face full of pimples.

Another basketball game "down the drain." *(handwritten)*

A Dad who always says "No." *(handwritten)*

What would life be like without trials? We'll never know. They are as inevitable as rainy days after you washed the car. Besides, they really are very useful. You can tell a lot about people by the way they handle those roadblocks.

Some get mad. Buddy slammed the tire iron into the back rear wheel. He was upset because an inconsiderate nail caused the tire to go flat. I timed him. He takes 23½ minutes to change a tire when he's fuming. When he's relaxed, he does it in 12 minutes flat.

Some pout. Judy wanted to date Byron. But mother said no. She didn't know him, and besides, she'd been out every night that week. Judy stayed home all right—in her room. She refused to eat or talk to anyone for two days.

Some withdraw. "But Mom, I can't go to school looking like this." Andrea had a point—right on the end of her nose. A great, big, red pimple.

Some attack. "He's got to be the clumsiest oaf that ever lived. All I said was 'Hurry up and pass the toast,' and he knocked over the milk. Now what will I wear?"

Some freeze: a fight; some threats; a dare, and the dust and fists begin to fly. Somebody should help Mom. Someone needs to talk some sense to Dad. But it won't be Charlie. He's flat on his bed with a pillow on his head.

Some grow. *A pop quiz? You've got to be kidding, Mr. Blair. No reason to fight it,* Linda reasoned. *Might as well see how well I'm doing. That could be a real help for preparing for the mid-term, too.*

Trials can clobber you or they can clear the trails for bigger challenges.

It's all up to you.

Also check out: Anger, Disobedience, Doubt, Failure, Fear, Frustration, Griping, Illness, Peer Pressure, Self-control, Success, Victory, Worry.

56

Uncertainty

"And the witness is this, that God has given us eternal life, and this life is in His Son. He who has the Son has the life; he who does not have the Son of God does not have the life. These things I have written to you who believe in the name of the Son of God, in order that you may know that you have eternal life" (1 John 5:11-13).

Ginny was surprised to learn the subject of the debate for English III class: "The Existence of God, Myth or Reality?"

There were to be six members on each side. Those chosen were exempt from doing a term paper for the semester. That was a consolation, but debating wasn't one of Ginny's strong points. She sure wanted the best arguments presented for the "Reality" side, however.

The debaters were finally chosen. Cliff Rangle was to be captain of the pro-God team. His father taught at the local Bible college. Besides Cliff, there were Sherry and Bernie (both pastors' kids), Mark (a new Christian), Stephanie (president of the church youth group), and Ginny.

"We'll blow them away," Cliff kept saying. But Ginny was worried—not about herself. She knew she believed in God. But all the same, proving it in class would not be simple.

"I mean, we can't deal with theory and subjective

214 Devotions with a Difference

speculations alone," she protested to the team. When it came time to divide up the research topics, Ginny was given "Christian Certainties, What We Know for Sure."

Ginny's study on the subject kept leading her back to the book of First John. But she knew that source wouldn't convince the class skeptics in the way a mathematical formula or a scientific axiom would. However, she could claim she had tested those promises in the laboratory of her own life and found them to be true.

The day of the debate, Ginny felt they were all prepared. But no one was "blown away." Arguments from design, from creation, and from many other classical approaches were refined by both sides. When Ginny's turn came, she quietly began her introduction.

"The God that Christians worship can be studied through a written record of His words and deeds, which is called the Bible. There we have in black and white a historical account of this God's dealings with human beings. From Genesis to Revelation, this book is a drama that centers on God's Son, Jesus Christ, whom Christians believe to be God coming to earth in human form. This incredible claim needs to be seriously studied by anyone who wants to know if God exists."

Then Ginny gave a listing of twenty-four promises that all Christians can be sure of from the testimony of the Bible and the witness of the many people down through the ages who believed them. Here are some of the points she covered:

We know that God dwells in us (1 John 4:12-13).

We know that God loves us (1 John 4:16-17).

We know we have eternal life (1 John 5:12-13).

We know that God hears our prayers (1 John 5:14-15).

We know that we belong to God (1 John 5:19-20).

The debate ended in a near draw. Out of the forty students in the class, only one changed from her previous position.

Jackie spent the rest of the afternoon talking to Ginny. She was intrigued by the confidence that Ginny and the rest of her team portrayed in what they were saying. Several days later, she prayed to commit her life to Christ and began her own faith adventure of knowing the certainty that she was a child of God.

All that work and only one was convinced. But Ginny thought it was worth it. After all, Jackie was now her best friend, and a new Christian.

Also check out: Atheism, Compromise, Creation, Doubt, Judgment, Peer Pressure, Zeal.

57

Ungratefulness

"And as He entered a certain village, there met Him ten leprous men, who stood at a distance; and they raised their voices, saying, 'Jesus, Master, have mercy on us!' . . . Now one of them, when he saw that he had been healed, turned back, glorifying God with a loud voice, and he fell on his face at His feet, giving thanks to Him. And he was a Samaritan. And Jesus answered and said, 'Were there not ten cleansed? But the nine—where are they? Were none found who turned back to give glory to God, except this foreigner?'" (Luke 17:12-13, 15-18).

Hey, Gregory. Yes, you. Come here a moment. What do you expect to happen tomorrow? No, I'm not playing games. Yes, I realize you're a busy boy. But this won't take long. Give me all the particulars. I'll write them here in my notebook. Yes, everything. OK?

Get up. Right.

Clean up. Check.

Breakfast.

Go to school.

Have lunch. So far, so good.

More classes.

Baseball practice.

Play TV games with brother, Lance.

Dinner.

Family devotions. Excellent.

Homework. Good boy.

And bed.

So, that does it? Nothing special. Just an average day in the life of one Gregory Morgan. Oh, wait a minute, please. Let's go over that list again.

Get up. Let's see, your father, who gets up an hour earlier, will have to come into your room at least three times to shake you awake. Why? So you won't be late to algebra again.

Clean up. Remember that shirt you wanted to wear today? Tonight your mother will be up late doing laundry so you'll have it clean and ready for your fabulous body.

Breakfast. Someone will have to stand in the kitchen watching the waffle iron while the rest of you eat. Guess who? Good old Mom. And they say it's going to rain. So Dad will be giving you a lift even though it means he has to wait a half hour longer.

School. Did you know that Mrs. Robinson, your English teacher, has an ill husband in the hospital? But she keeps her smile while listening to hundreds of recitations of epic poetry all day.

Remember that seventy-five cents you spent for lunch at the cafeteria? Just a few coins to throw out to you, but it represents some hard struggles for your dad down at that pressure cooker he calls an office.

Baseball. Let's see: mitt, $55; shoes, $45; insurance, $10. And who comes to every game? I've seen the whole gang there at one time or another: Dad, Mom, your sister, and even your two-year-old brother.

And those TV games? They represent three days salary down the tubes, so to speak.

I hear you've got another huckleberry pie coming. That's not your mother's favorite activity, but you went on and on about that other one, so—.

Devotions. So God sent His Son. Are those words so familiar to you that you take them for granted? Have you taken much time to think about Him lately? Sure, I know how it is. There's so much to do and so little time.

Homework. You do remember that your sister's been typing away on the term paper for you? And isn't that something that your friend Billy is going to pick up those reference books for you at the library, and that comes after you called him a jerk for ordering the wrong kind of hamburger for you? How about it, Greg?

So, your average, ordinary day comes to its end. Bed. Clean sheets. Soft pillow. Homemade quilt. Everyone just doing his duty, hey Greg? Well, what about it? Don't you think a few thank-yous are in order?

Also check out: Apathy, Boredom, Criticism, Depression, Family, Friends, Frustration, Greed, Griping, Humility, Jealousy, Love, Pettiness, Selfishness.

58

Victory

"But thanks be to God, who gives us the victory through our Lord Jesus Christ. Therefore, my beloved brethren, be steadfast, immovable, always abounding in the work of the Lord, knowing that your toil is not in vain in the Lord" (1 Corinthians 15:57-58).

Barry started smoking when he was fourteen. At seventeen he decided to stop. It wasn't that easy. But after six long months of sweating it out, he kicked the habit. No more yellow teeth. No more bad breath. No more ashes burning holes in his car upholstery. Sweet victory.

Linda knew that a girl of sixteen shouldn't be afraid of the dark. But that knowledge didn't keep her heart from pounding and her knees from shaking when she crossed the church parking lot to reach her car.

For years she was terrified to be left alone in the house. She wouldn't even take out the garbage after dark. Linda realized there was cause for a young girl to be cautious, but she didn't want to be forever bound by her paralyzing fears. She talked it out, read about it, prayed about it, and finally let go. Now she's finding victory.

Victory isn't merely for a few super Christians. The power to overcome is available to all who follow Christ.

Here are a few guidelines that might help you to get started toward that goal of victory:

First, know your enemy. It sounds simple, but it isn't. Kelly has begged and begged her parents to get her out of P.E. She says Miss Mitchell is cruel to her and the class is too strenuous. Actually, Kelly has a severe struggle with undressing and showering in front of the rest of the girls. Her enemy is her own view of who she is and how she looks.

Second, expect to win. Some people plan to fail. Others don't plan at all. Kelly got desperate enough that she took her mother's advice. She studied the Scripture about God's direct involvement in creation. She learned that He doesn't make rejects or seconds. She took a short course in anatomy to better understand her body. She saved her money for a charm course and carried her frame straighter. Meanwhile, she stuck to P.E. until she could see some sign of progress.

Third, rely on God's strength. If you've never been ashamed of your looks, you probably don't have any idea what Kelly went through. It depressed her to stand in front of a mirror, because she'd only see those imperfections she so disliked. But through her tears and her prayers, she changed her request from, "Lord, change me now!" to "Help me to like myself as I am."

Fourth, don't quit trying until you win. Stay with your original plan until a better plan replaces it or you achieve what you set out to accomplish.

Kelly is still one of the most modest girls at school. That's OK. She is one year older now and ten pounds lighter, and she found a new way to style her hair. She doesn't pretend that she'll ever be a model, but she does like herself. Not only that, but she's also friends with Miss Mitchell and looks forward to P.E. For Kelly, that's real victory.

Also check out: Competition, Compromise, Frustration, Purpose, Self-worth, Self-control, Trauma, Trials.

59

Violence

"And the Lord had regard for Abel and his offering; but for Cain and for his offering He had no regard. So Cain became very angry and his countenance fell. Then the Lord said to Cain, 'Why are you so angry? And why has your countenance fallen? If you do well, will not your countenance be lifted up? And if you do not do well, sin is crouching at the door; and its desire is for you, but you must master it.' And Cain told Abel his brother. And it came about when they were in the field, that Cain rose up against Abel his brother and killed him" (Genesis 4:4b-8).

Butch and Sunny loved to spend a week at Grandpa's each summer. He was the last of a different era. A bearskin rug, a giant elk-head trophy, and an old Winchester graced his simple mountain cabin as naturally as his pioneer stories late in the night.

One day while Grandpa fished for dinner down at the lake, the boys sorted through his gun collection. He had some rare antiques, but they were all crammed in a disorganized pile in the back of his coat closet. He had rifles, pistols, shotguns, and flintlocks, but the boys' favorite was the old, heavy Colt .45 and holster. There it was hidden behind a genuine Sharps buffalo rifle.

But the boys discovered an added bonanza this year. Tossed aside in an old cigar box were some bullets he had picked up at an auction. They searched for some that would fit the .45. They found only one.

Shortly after they shoved the slug into one of the chambers, they heard a roar coming from the canyon. Dirt-bikers. Grandpa would be furious.

Butch grabbed the pistol and yelled, "Come on, Sunny, let's give those trespassers a real scare." They raced down to the creek bank and reached the trail before the bikers.

"What are you going to do? Shoot at a tire?" Sunny asked.

"Naw, that's too risky. I'll shoot above them into the trees."

At the sight of two husky teens waving a pistol in the air, the violators quickly slipped off the trail and into the wild huckleberries. A blast rang out. Ten feet above the frightened riders, branches flew. Butch stumbled backward several feet but still clutched the smoking weapon. The boys laughed all the way back to the cabin.

Meanwhile, just over the hill at the Montgomery house, which nestled in a grove of Jeffrey pines, Angela and Amy giggled as they ate cereal at the kitchen table. All of a sudden they heard a sharp bump against the wall of their house on the north, then an immediate bang against the south kitchen wall. Their mother ran in and said, "What happened?"

"Oh, I guess something's beating on our walls," said six-year-old Angela.

"Mom, look!" cried out four-year-old Amy, "a hole right in our wall."

That night their father dug out the slug. "Right through wood siding, six inches of insulation and interior wall, across a fourteen-foot room, and two feet above Angela and Amy into the redwood paneling. That's some trick."

Butch and Sunny received a $500 fine and were put on a year's probation. They got off pretty cheap. Most of us can recall similar kinds of situations that ended with a senseless, untimely death.

The potential for that kind of violence is always with us in this fallen world. But there's another tragic violence that causes as much pain and should be feared as the murderer it is.

We worry so much about the safety of our bodies, while our souls and spirits rot and decay. Jesus gave a pointed challenge to us safety and pleasure seekers: "For what will a man be profited, if he gains the whole world, and forfeits his soul?" (Matthew 16:26*b*).

Jesus is looking for a few brave souls who will volunteer service in a war He's already won. There are plenty of mop-up battles yet to wage. Guns won't help you, though. You'll need a tougher kind of weapon. "Put on the full armor of God, that you may be able to stand firm against the schemes of the devil. For our struggle is not against flesh and blood, but against the rulers, against the powers, against the world forces of this darkness, against the spiritual forces of wickedness in the heavenly places" (Ephesians 6:11-12).

If you're interested, Ephesians 6 gives a rundown on some of the battle tactics. There are many of us out here trying to keep faithful, plugging in there to the glorious finale. How about it? We could use a youthful regular like you who's all primed and ready to go for the adventure of his life.

Also check out: Anger, Boldness, Death, Fear, Judgment, Self-control, Suicide, Trauma, Victory, Zeal.

60

Vocation

"And He gave some as apostles, and some as prophets, and some as evangelists, and some as pastors and teachers, for the equipping of the saints for the work of service, to the building up of the body of Christ; until we all attain to the unity of the faith, and of the knowledge of the son of God, to a mature man, to the measure of the stature which belongs to the fulness of Christ" (Ephesians 4:11-13).

What are you going to be when you grow up?

    age 3—"A garbage man, 'cause he drives a big truck."

    age 6—"A cowboy."

    age 9—"A baseball free agent."

    age 12—"A nuclear physicist."

    age 15—"Uh, well, I don't really know."

    age 18—"What do you mean? I *am* grown up!"

Most teens don't have any idea what they want to do with their lives. And if they could, they'd be quite surprised to peek into the future and see what they finally settle on as occupations.

Abraham didn't plan to be a wandering Aramean. God just pushed him out of his hometown and sent him on his way.

Moses was content as a shepherd. At an age when most

229

people have long been retired, he met God in a burning bush.

Amos loved to farm, but God's prophetic words burned even deeper in his heart.

Who would have thought the young boy driven from his home of Jerusalem would one day be prime minister of a foreign country? It happened to Daniel.

Jesus never hesitated to turn fishermen, tax collectors, or revolutionary fighters into evangelists or preachers.

Statistics show that the average college student changes his career goals three times before graduating. So dream big. Consider all the options. Experiment to find what things you can do well. Do you work best with people, machines, ideas, or space to create?

Seek the best training you can possibly afford. Soak up all the knowledge in a general field you feel drawn to. As you begin to eliminate some of your wide range of choices and narrow down to a probable, select few, coordinate your job, school, and various other activities to expand your experience in that area.

Set a goal of craftsmanship. Whether your expertise is cabinet-making, social work, or medical research, excellence should guide your efforts as you seek to honor our Lord in everything you do.

And don't be surprised if one day, when you think you have the matter all settled, you feel a divine tap on the shoulder, calling you to something else.

Also check out: Family, Future, Grades, Happiness, Illness, Marriage, Materialism, Purpose, Success.

61

Worry

"But Martha was distracted with all her preparations; and she came up to Him, and said, 'Lord, do You not care that my sister has left me to do all the serving alone? Then tell her to help me.' But the Lord answered and said to her, 'Martha, Martha, you are worried and bothered about so many things; but only a few things are necessary, really only one, for Mary has chosen the good part, which shall not be taken away from her'" (Luke 10:40-42).

There is always something to worry about.

How does this look? What did I forget? Who is going to be there? What if they don't like me? What if I don't like them? What if he doesn't ask me? What if he does ask me? What if she says no? What if she says yes? When will I get a new car? Will I get a job this summer? What if I hate chemistry? What if I love chemistry?

Jesus said we worry too much about the wrong things. How do you decide which worries are more important?

1. List all those things that now crowd your mind with attention and concern. Be specific.

    a. _____

    b. _____

c. _____

d. _____

2. Reread the above list. Which of those are likely to still be concerns of yours by tonight (x), by tomorrow (t), by next week (w), by next month (m), a year from now (l), five years from now (5), on into eternity (E). Place an appropriate symbol by each worry on your list.

The longer the effect on your life, the more important the concern. For instance, "I worry that I really don't know God at all" is an obvious "E."

3. Now divide the worries into two categories.

    A. Concerns that are totally out of my hands (such as, "I hope I don't get drafted"). Release those to God's divine intervention.

    B. Concerns I can deal with. By each of these place a date on which you will make a decision on the matter (such as, "By Friday I'll decide which jobs to apply for").

Now, worry only about those items you have marked "Today." Relax about all the rest. You'll have more time (and maybe more insight) to handle them at the later date.

By analyzing your worries this way, you'll find some that aren't worth bothering about. If they won't even affect your life past tonight, maybe they're not worth another thought at all.

When you find a conflict between worries and wonder which to deal with first, always choose the one with the longer-lasting effect. That's what Mary did in the above story. She had two concerns, hospitality or listening to every word of Jesus for the short time He was there, and she chose the right one. So can you.

Also check out: Boldness, Competition, Depression, Doubt, Fear, Guilt, Illness, Judgment, Selfishness, Shyness, Success, Trials.

62

Zeal ✦

"For it is superfluous for me to write to you about this ministry to the saints; for I know your readiness, of which I boast about you to the Macedonians, namely, that Achaia has been prepared since last year, and your zeal has stirred up most of them" (2 Corinthians 9:1-2).

You need zeal.

What?

I said "zeal."

What's that?

Zeal is that rare enthusiasm that combines with ardent passion to see that a thing gets done. It should be a characteristic of every Christian.

Elijah had it.

He gathered all the people of Israel at Mount Carmel to demonstrate the power of God. Hundreds of priests of Baal were there to defend their Phoenician god's honor. They danced around a huge pile of firewood in hopes that Baal would light it. He couldn't, of course.

Then came Elijah's turn. He heaped on gallons of water until the whole area looked like a flash flood. Then he called on God to light the fire—just once, in front of thousands of witnesses. That's zeal.

235

Jesus had it.

He was shocked to see how the Temple was misused. Instead of finding worshipers, He found sheep stalls, banks, haggling inspectors, and merchants. Jesus grabbed a corded whip and began swinging. Animals were driven out, merchants fled, tables were overturned. That's zeal.

Philip had it.

He was the first successful preacher to the Samaritans. Many of them received the truth of Christ. Then he found himself in the desert, answering one Ethiopian's questions. The man received God's truth. Then Philip traveled to the coastland and preached the whole way. He had zeal. Without it there is no spiritual progress.

Katie had zeal.

Nine months ago her high school youth group consisted of three members: the pastor's two sons and Katie.

She began to pray every day that the group would grow. She wanted others to come to know Christ. She made a list of all the teens in their small area that she thought they might reach. There were twenty-four altogether. Then, she asked the adults in her church to "adopt a kid" in prayer. Each was given a name or two.

Whenever she could, Katie took advantage of opportunities to tell one of those acquaintances about the youth group and what they were planning. She invited them to attend and even offered rides.

Her parents caught her enthusiasm, too. They invited some of the families over for dinner and tried to cultivate some friendships.

By the end of nine months, Katie had been responsible

for seventeen out of those twenty-four attending at least one youth activity. They now had eleven regular, active members.

Phenomenal growth? It all depends on where you're coming from.

Phenomenal zeal? You'd better believe it!

Also check out: Apathy, Boldness, Boredom, Depression, Doubt, Fear, Love, Purpose, Restitution, Success, Trials, Uncertainty, Victory.